12 2.71

These are the makings of a counter culture, a way of life espoused by the young and opposed in many ways to the values of the older generation—a culture analyzed by writers like Theodore Roszak *(The Making of a Counter Culture),* Charles Reich *(The Greening of America),* and now by Robert L. Johnson, campus pastor at the University of North Carolina.

Drawing on his experience with college students, Johnson analyzes the reasons for the counter culture, its present manifestations, and its significance for the Christian faith. And from his graduate study in Christian mysticism and in Buddhism he is able to offer a critique from a theological perspective. He encourages the church to rediscover its mystical heritage, to come to grips with the developing counter culture, and to help shape it according to the Christian vision of the kingdom of God.

Counter Culture and the Vision of God

Counter Culture and the Vision of God

Robert L. Johnson

Foreword by Tom Driver

AUGSBURG PUBLISHING HOUSE

Minneapolis, Minnesota

COUNTER CULTURE AND THE VISION OF GOD

Quotation from "Blowing My Mind at Harvard" by Larry L. King reprinted by permission of Larry L. King.

Quotation from "Judaism and the Death of God," by Richard Rubenstein reprinted by permission of *Playboy* magazine.

Quotations from *The Glass Bead Game (Magister Ludi)* by Hermann Hesse, translated by Richard and Clara Winston, foreword by Theodore Ziolkowski, copyright © 1969 by Holt, Rinehart and Winston, Inc., reprinted by permission of Holt, Rinehart and Winston, Inc.

Quotation from *The Uncompleted Past* by Martin Duberman, copyright © 1964, 65, 66, 67, 68 by Martin Duberman, reprinted by permission of The Sterling Lord Agency.

Quotations from *The Myth of the Machine: The Pentagon of Power,* copyright © 1964, 1970, by Harcourt Brace Jovanovich, Inc., reprinted with their permission.

Quotation from "The Dry Salvages" in *Four Quartets,* copyright © 1943 by T. S. Eliot, reprinted by permission of Harcourt Brace Jovanovich, Inc.

Quotation from *Systematic Theology* by Paul Tillich, reprinted by permission of University of Chicago Press.

Quotation from *The Vision of God* by Kenneth E. Kirk reprinted by permission.

Quotation from "Who'll Stop the Rain," by John Fogerty, reprinted by permission.

Scripture quotations are from the Revised Standard Version of the Bible, copyright 1946 and 1952 by the Division of Christian Education of the National Council of Churches, and are used by permission.

1636386

Contents

Foreword

Robert L. Johnson's book about the counter-culture is written as a sympathetic and discerning report. It comes from one who works among and loves students, and is addressed to those who are bewildered by the alien style of youth. Johnson knows that the style is not all froth, and he seeks to interpret the spirit that grows long hair and looks askance at the tradition of high seriousness.

A reader would be mistaken, however, to regard this book solely as a commentary on those "foreigners" who are our own children. It is not, after all, as if our children had learned little from us, nor as if we ourselves did not have the same appetites that lead our "youngers" to adopt the very behavior we choose to regard with suspicion.

The motif that is common to us all is alienation. To be alienated from nature, culture, institutions,

9

neighbor, family, and self is, to a degree, the universal human condition; but it has grown to the proportions of a plague since the rise of industrialism and has become even more severe with the advent of technology. Hegel, Kierkegaard, Marx, Feuerbach, Nietzsche, Freud—almost all the great 19th-century thinkers—talked about it. Bertolt Brecht and many others tried to turn it into an aesthetic principle. Totalitarianisms use it to control the masses.

In the first half of our century, Western civilization had twice to defend itself against barbarianism, and between the two World Wars it suffered severe economic depression. These crises had the temporary effect of uniting our civilization against adversaries, and this produced an apparent diminution of the feeling of alienation. T. S. Eliot and others rediscovered "the tradition," while "crisis theology" turned to a modern form of orthodoxy. To paraphrase Eliot in "The Wasteland," we shored up our fragments against our ruin. By every overt standard we won. Our governments, our economy, and our schools survived. But spiritually, without a doubt, we lost. The fragments are now pulverized.

The period of depression and World War is the period which gave birth and formation to most of those who are now educators, pastors, legislators, managers—in short, the leaders of the "established" society. And we of that generation do tend to operate out of something like what Charles Reich has called Consciousness II. Our avowed aims and values are mostly liberal, but our posture remains that of shoring up fragments. We are deeply alienated people—most of all from ourselves.

About 1960 the culture changed. John F. Kennedy was no more a man of the new culture than was Pope John XXIII; but, like his namesake, he was prepared to let change happen. Anyway, he could not have stopped it, for it was more cultural than political.

The younger generation is no less alienated than its elders. The difference is that it is more aware of the alienation and is prepared to act it out. In this, it has a distinct psychological advantage, for awareness and dramatization yield transcendence, and transcendence is psychological power. So true is this that the older generation often feels itself impotent in the face of filial nonchalance. And there lies the danger. For feelings of impotence, as Rollo May has recently reminded us, are an open invitation to outbursts and strategies of repressive tyranny. It is when I feel weak that I am most likely to act like Genghis Khan; and the closer the FBI comes to the methods of a secret police, the more one knows that the FBI feels insecure.

It is therefore of utmost importance that the older generation identify *within itself* the very same feelings and longings that move the young to smoke pot, read Herman Hesse, sit light with received versions of history, cluster in groups of love, hear music as tribal incantation, and lie down in the doorways of draft boards. If we cannot identify these motifs within ourselves, we shall not know where the young derive their strength, and we shall act from desperate powerlessness.

I do not speak of vicarious identification but of self-recognition. Woodstock—on its good and bad sides, in its love and its commercialism—is the fantasy of the parents who stayed at home. As Eric Bentley once said, in scathing tone, the East Village is Scarsdale on its night out. The trouble is not that that's true but that Scarsdale will not admit it.

The name of the game I propose is awareness and self-recognition. I therefore hope that Robert L. Johnson's book will be read, not as a window into something going on "over there," but as a mirror of something "in here," a revelation of the curves and undulations that are the alienated part of the square.

TOM F. DRIVER
Professor of Theology and Literature
Union Theological Seminary, New York

Preface

The seeds for this book were planted about four years ago when, as a campus minister at the University of North Carolina, I first began to take note of a growing interest among students and faculty for what I then described as esoteric and mystical groups. One of these groups asked to use our building for several meetings, and I was frankly incredulous at the serious attention with which a long and obscure lecture on the teaching of Meher Baba was received. (Baba was a Sufi mystic who claimed to be the latest avatar of God and followed a long discipline of silence. He established a meditation center near Myrtle Beach in South Carolina.)

All of this occurred at the time of a marked decline in student response in both Protestant worship and theology, several years after the great civil rights movement, and in the midst of the severe political disenchantment of 1967-68. My own theological training had conditioned me to view such developments with a jaundiced eye, suspicious of syncretism, gnosticism, and students who used discussion of "the world religions" to evade an encounter with their own Christian heritage. I was gladly ensconced in the Christian realism of the Niebuhrs, with my ministry focused more on power politics and corporate responsibility than on the cultivation of any form of interior piety. I viewed anything of a "mystical" tinge as a historical "cop-out," something reserved for elderly English ladies in tennis shoes —shades of Madame Blavatsky and theosophy!

This bias gradually eroded as I encountered more and more students who were intellectually alert and socially responsible, yet also very much into mystical literature or the Romantic poets. I noted the revival William Blake enjoyed among English majors and the eager reception accorded the Tolkien legends of the hobbit. In the course of examining graduate schools for a year of study, I travelled to Harvard in the spring of 1967, and was quickly informed by a law student that Herman Hesse's *Siddartha* was very much "in." So I read *Siddartha,* found it somewhat dull, and remained quite puzzled by the interest it had generated among the young.

All these puzzlements prepared me for a year of study (thanks to the Danforth Foundation) and provided the impetus for me to focus my work on the history of religions with special attention to Buddhist thought. I chose Harvard because of my great admiration for the late dean of the Divinity School, Samuel H. Miller, and the reputation of The Center for the Study of World Religions there. This center, under the imaginative direction of Wilfred C. Smith, a specialist in Islamic studies, offered a community within which the knowledge gained from the classroom and the library could be tested out against living representatives of the major faith traditions and, in this way, a cogent and sympathetic understanding could be formed. In addition, the year at Harvard allowed me two semesters of study with Masatoshi Nagatomi in the development of Buddhist thought from India through China and Japan; a provocative course with Raymond Pannikar, a Roman Catholic scholar from Benares, on "Atheism: Christian and Buddhist"; and an opportunity to participate in a seminar with Richard R. Niebuhr on language and Christian discourse.

Probably my most rewarding work at Harvard was done under the guidance of George H. Williams. As a church historian who valued the work of the early fathers—especially in their emphasis on the human will—and as one who had probed the mystic dimensions of Luther's faith and Luther's ties with the great Dominican mystics of the 14th century, he was able to spare me much grief in the murky quest for the residue of Protestant mysticism. Indeed there were days when I waited outside Williams' office in the lower depths of the Widener Library to begin our reading course, that I found myself ready to abandon the mystic quest and go back to "Christian realism." At the point of retreat, however, I was always bolstered by Williams' sense of the catholicity of the church and his regard for movements and dimensions of the faith now in eclipse. I had never so fully appreciated how desperately contemporary Christian theology needs the comprehensive wisdom of the historian.

Having completed the year at Harvard, I needed another year for much of what I had studied in the area of mysticism to make imaginative and emotive connection with the forces of the emerging counter culture. So much intervened in that period to reinforce those basic impulses that first led me to examine the mystic phenomena: a deepening political disenchantment, growing drug use, the rediscovery of our intimate links with the natural world through both ecology and sensitivity groups, a renewed sense for me personally of the need for corporate worship as an ultimate horizon against which cultures die and new constellations of meaning are conceived.

I have observed these developments from the perpective of a campus minister on one of our oldest and liveliest state universities. As one of my earliest mentors in campus ministry once observed, "Trying to sustain a Christian community on a university campus is like a hen laying an egg on an escalator!" It *is* something like that. Too often, those of us who serve in campus ministry have bemoaned our "marginal" status—marginal both to the power centers of church and university—without fully appreciating the benefits of our marginality. We work in a critically important place from which to observe student alienation from established religion and education. We see the poverty of family life, the hunger for sensory experience, the sometimes desperate, sometimes comic groupings for a viable and coherent faith. At several points we have been called to participate in the two central thrusts of the counter culture: its radical prophetic element and its mystic communal element. We have been exposed to alternate styles of learning and worshiping that have shaped our understanding and appropriation of the Christian faith. In the process we have been forced to abandon many of our conventional programs, our faddistic theological slogans, our narrow sectarianism. Sometimes we have learned against our will of the impulses for health in the youth culture. We live close to their despair, their spontaneity, their fragile sense of beauty, their redeeming humor and innocence.

One incentive for me to write this book has come out of the distress occasioned by my colleagues in both church and university who find it all too easy to dismiss the promise of the youth culture without seriously confronting the issues raised by it. Neither church nor university is in any position to minimize the potentialities of a genuine shift in cultural allegiance on the part of the young. We are still dealing with an emerging phenomenon. There is no doubt much simplistic and escapist thinking in what is loosely called "counter culture." But there is also the possibility of a major turn in human understanding and the option of quite fresh appropriations of both faith and learning.

Let me express a final word of gratitude to those who make up a most intimate and happy household and who have informed all that follows: my wife, Barbara, and our sons, Paul and Christopher. While cherishing our life together, they have gladly opened their lives to a larger community of friends and strangers and have always provided me with that grounding in trust which encourages new explorations.

18

1

COUNTER CULTURE:
THE REALITY OF
A REVOLUTION

Billy had a framed prayer on his office wall which
expressed his method for keeping going, even though
he was unenthusiastic about living. A lot of patients
who saw the prayer on Billy's wall told him that it
helped *them* to keep going, too. It went like this:

God Grant Me
The Serenity to Accept
The Things I Cannot Change,
Courage
To Change the Things I Can,
And Wisdom Always
To Tell the
Difference.

Among the things Billy Pilgrim could not change
were the past, the present, and the future.

—Kurt Vonnegut, *Slaughterhouse Five*

Counter culture. The term had scarcely been in-
troduced in university and media circles before
critics attempted to deny its reality and friends
hailed it as the new establishment. While the

phenomenon of counter culture remains problematic, there is nonetheless sufficient literature before us to indicate that something genuinely fresh is emerging from the youth culture. Parents, educators, youth counsellors, and politicians are alert to the distinctive nature of young Americans. The young indeed seem to be dropping out of established traditions and values and turning in to strange and sometimes threatening sources of enlightenment.

Many of the young would hesitate to describe themselves as caught up in a "counter culture" with all the historical pretensions that entails. They would, however, indicate the points at which they find themselves alienated from the values of their parents and the family styles and work styles of earlier generations. They vividly witness to the impact of war and television and drugs and political frustration on their lives, and confess their hunger for new sources of meaning and direction.

Believers in the Promise

There are adult observers who have laid the groundwork for a critical encounter with the forces generating the counter culture. Students of adolescent behavior such as Kenneth Keniston, Edgar Z. Friedenberg, and Paul Goodman have forcefully portrayed the dilemmas of a prolonged adolescence without meaningful work or a sense of community.[1] Keniston has studied both alienated dropouts and committed radicals and indicated the points at which prevailing values are rejected by these young people.

While these observers have reported on the special stresses of the young in America, the first substantial case for a counter culture was advanced by Theodore Roszak in *The Making of a Counter Culture: Reflections on the technocratic society and its youthful opposition*.[2] Roszak, writing out of an academic context on the West coast, realized how difficult it would be to establish the reality of a movement for an alternate culture. He noted in the preface to his book that some of his colleagues had almost convinced him that neither "the Romantic movement" nor "the Renaissance" had ever existed. And if such historically remote judgments were questionable, how dare Roszak or anyone else assert that now, at the end of a turbulent decade clouded in tragic ambiguities, there was an underground cultural stream of substantial character that signaled a shift in human consciousness?

To be sure, Roszak knew he was dealing with a *movement* in process, a movement without central organization, ideology, or common manifesto. He described a "cultural constellation" that included "the interests of our college-age and adolescent young in the psychology of alienation, oriental mysticism, psychedelic drugs, and communitarian experiments." [3] And he acknowledged that this constellation of forces needed much maturing before it could settle on priorities and develop enduring social cohesion. But he did establish the proximate range of the counter culture: it was largely a youth culture excluding the more conservative young, the Kennedy style liberals, and the militant blacks. Roszak noted the movement of the children of technocracy away from established religion, politics, and work styles toward nomadic groups celebrating mystic rites, finding a "counterfeit identity" in drugs, and abandoning reform politics for the creation of subcommunities governed by the participants.

This shift of youthful energies toward the creation of an alternative life style has also been the subject of Charles Reich's attention. Reich, a young professor of law at Yale, has passionately argued in his bestseller, *The Greening of America,* that a revolution is underway—a revolution unlike those of the past which had been marked by terror and violence.[4] Reich's version is a revolution of consciousness rather than a revolution through political struggle.

Reich spells out this transformation in three stages of consciousness. Consciousness I is the consciousness of small-town America, wedded to the work ethic, resistant to change, loyal to existing institutions. Consciousness II is the consciousness of the liberal reformers from the New Deal through the Kennedys, who have only served to strengthen the power of the corporate state over the life of the individual and thus betrayed the American dream of maximal freedom. Consciousness III affirms the natural goodness of man, a quest for transcendence, liberation from conventional restraints, and a determination to return technology to the service of human ends.

While Reich's book has been subjected to a variety of clever "put-downs" by leading journals (e.g., "The Fuzzing of America," "The Greening of Charles Reich," "The Third Reich"), he maintains an admirable posture of quiet confidence and non-defensiveness. He has openly reminded his critics of the weak points in the counter culture and the difficult areas in which learning must occur. While his advocacy of the revolution in consciousness has led him into sometimes simplistic, sometimes ludicrous expressions, he manages to communicate the important point that the heart of Consciousness III is "not in the shape of its pants, but in its liberation, its change of goals, its search for self, its doctrines of honesty and responsibility." [5]

Consciousness III will triumph, according to Reich, not through violent confrontation or the usual channels of political reform, but simply through the shift in cultural allegiances. He has stated better than most the futility of pursuing change through political struggle. He avoids further political frustration by focusing on a new target for revolutionary hopes: "one does not fight a machine head-on, one pulls out the plug." [6] Reich calls us to turn from a political revolution that cannot succeed to a cultural revolution that will establish a new system of values and a new community. Like many others, he proclaims the end of liberal reformism.

For both Reich and Roszak, the counter culture represents a revolt against the corporate state, its rationalized bureaucracy, and its pragmatic ethic. It includes all those, young and old, who have sought to extricate themselves from the machine-like grasp of technocracy and a restricted sense of selfhood. It is a coalition struggling with what Roszak sees as the dialectic of liberation represented by Herbert Marcuse and Norman O. Brown: radical politics and mystical salvation.

While there are considerable differences between the judgments on the youth culture drawn by Roszak and Reich, they both point to the alienated quality of that culture and its struggle to come forth with alternate life styles. Together they have been bold in affirming the possibility of a real option before the binds of technocracy.

Reich is the more sanguine; he sees the life style of the young radically altering the direction of American history "like flowers pushing up through a concrete pavement." [7] Roszak is both more sober and more desperate in acknowledging the capacity of technocracy to absorb discontent and cultural deviation.

Critical Reservations

The counter culture, as advocated by Roszak and Reich, has encountered a barrage of criticism from social scientists, journalists, and historians. It is judged by some to be a creation of old radicals and tired Bohemians. While the counter culture is said to be generated by the youth culture, these critics note the prominence of another generation in its leadership: Marx and Marcuse, Freud and Norman O. Brown, William Blake and the Eastern mystics. They ask for evidence of substantially new ideological and aesthetic creations from the counter culture.

Others have noted the obvious points of continuity between the present counter culture and the Romantic movement going back to Rousseau and Coleridge. The celebration of feeling, the cult of intensive experience, the return to nature, the opposition to hierarchical patterns of community are all present in the revolt of the young. Coleridge can be seen as a pioneer in drug experimentation, and as one who rejected theological "proofs" reached by discursive reason and cultivated the receptive, subjective side of human understanding. This "Romantic" label suggests for most Americans a dreamy, emotional temperament appropriate for adolescents, utopians, and recluses. While the term can be used with greater integrity in the history of art, it carries a distinctly pejorative connotation in both the academic and theological communities. Thus, social scientists of the liberal establishment and theologians of the neo-orthodox school find it possible to dismiss the counter culture because of its romantic elements and its inadequate view of man's tragic character. Unfortunately, many critics will do so without careful reflection on the historical roots of what we call "Romanticism" and without examining the psychological dynamics underlying the search for an alternate culture.

More conservative critics of the counter culture have been content to acknowledge its presence as a "parallel culture"—sometimes disturbing, sometimes amusing—but a subculture that can be safely tolerated and even absorbed by the prevailing culture. It is seen as a youthful, leisure culture that offers no serious threat to established political or economic power. Indeed, it can even be tapped as a "youth market," which will be sold bell bottoms, rock festivals, and plastic peace symbols by the entrepreneurs of the corporate state.

This view of the counter culture is rudely shaken when the young attempt to act out a serious program of political liberation or infringe on the work and life styles of the corporate world. Nonetheless, this perspective of cultural absorption remains the most widely accepted way of dealing with the revolt of the young. The mass media have yet to produce a serious and honest treatment of the counter culture. The films produced in this direction are little more than tired clichés exploiting every sensational gimmick of the trade. Drugs, motorcycles, group sex, and violence inviting repression seem to constitute the counter culture as seen in the mass media. In a similar way, the "flower children" of Haight-Ashbury were quickly victimized by criminal elements and put on exhibit for the tourists. As Melvin Maddocks observed in *The Christian Science Monitor,* "The counter culture has become a kind of put-on—a style boutique for the youth market, a rip-off on itself." [8] Such treatment obscures the efforts of the young to escape from structures that would both tolerate and exploit them.

A more serious critique of the counter culture has come from those who would identify with the basic goals of human liberation and cultural transformation but who question Reich's strategy of "dropping out" of the technological system. Sociologists Peter and Brigitte Berger have argued that the cultural revolution advocated by Reich will only open up "the system" to a takeover by the least revolutionary forces in America. They argue that as upper-middle class youth abandon the corporate structures and blacks turn to separatist development, new social mobility will be afforded to lower-middle class whites. "In other words, precisely those classes that remain most untouched by what is considered to be the revolutionary tide in contemporary America face new prospects of upward social mobility." [9] The technological machine will continue to need skilled managers and the "liberated" young will only forfeit power for change in abandoning the system. The "greening" of America will really occur, the Bergers hold, when lower class whites find themselves in Consciousness III and show signs of wanting to "drop out" of the technocratic state. So far, they see no signs of such a movement.

The complex task of making some judgment about a phenomenon as loose and volatile as the present youth culture is further obscured by the tendency of some observers to view the movement analogically to previous deviations from the established norms of Western civilization.

So some would see the youth culture as a cyclical reappearance of the antinomian and Gnostic heresies of the third century. Christian critics seem especially given to such interpretations, which render them incapable of seeing *new* possibilities in a situation that is historically unique. One church journal recently expressed such a view:

> Repeatedly, throughout Western history the Gnostic stream of thought arises in times of rapid social change and stress. Communes and sects, complete with long hair and ragged clothes, appear almost overnight. When institutions arise that satisfy the common desire for order, these manifestations quickly become dormant to somehow survive until the next social upheaval.[10]

Such loose historical judgments serve only to reinforce the complacency of Christian people (especially clergy) that nothing new is expected of them and that they can rest easy in viewing the counter culture as an expression of *Weltschmerz* without noting the fact that the same kind of judgment surely must have been made of the "long hair" and "ragged clothes" of the primitive Christian counter culture, since it too emerged out of a time of "rapid social change and stress."

A more balanced and critical perspective has been provided by the rich humanism of Lewis Mumford. In his two-volume work, *The Myth of the Machine* and especially the second volume,

The Pentagon of Power, Mumford draws a bead on the same target as the youthful revolutionaries.[11] He examines a power complex in which political power is dependent on military power, productivity is yoked to profit, and propaganda is provided to bolster the authority of the elite.

Although Mumford believes that the manic aggrandizement of technocracy will end in Necropolis (The City of the Dead), he places considerable hope in the emergence of the youth culture. He sees there the beginnings of serious opposition to the values of "the megamachine," and the possibility of a genuine religious transformation. He sees among the young an apocalyptic awareness that cuts them off from the nurture of the old cultural values and propels them towards a new source of cultural sustenance. Harvard physicist, Gerald Holton, noted this awareness in a review of Mumford's *Pentagon of Power:*

> Indeed—some of the young people prefer to live as if the nuclear catastrophe had already occurred: among ruins without permanent shelter, without regular supply of food, without customs or habits except those improvised from day to day, without books or academic credentials, vocations or careers, or any source of knowledge except the experience of their own peers. They mass together and touch each other, and only in this way have any sense of security and continuity. The arts, too, mirror the derangement which the megamachine has produced in the human spirit, and thereby may help awaken man sufficiently to his actual plight.[12]

Holton has put his finger on a factor many critics of the counter culture have missed: the deep historic trauma experienced by the young, the crisis of hope that has led them to a detached relation to traditional values.

While Mumford has hopefully welcomed every sign of student dissent from the established values, he sees too much in the youth culture that remains within the grip of technocracy. He fears that the young will lose their underground character, and the movement will be powerless before a state committed to technological growth and military power. Impressed by the "warm sense of instant fellowship" evident at Woodstock, Mumford yet cautioned:

> The so-called Woodstock Festival was no spontaneous manifestation of joyous youth, but a strictly moneymaking enterprise, shrewdly calculated to exploit their rebellions, their adulations, their illusions. . . . With its mass mobilization of private cars and buses, its congestion of traffic en route, the Woodstock Festival mirrored and even grossly magnified the worst features of the system that many young rebels profess to reject, if not to destroy.[13]

He is likewise dubious before the argument of Roszak: "Roszak's evidences for anything that could be called a culture capable of counter-balancing the existing order are unsubstantial—and hardly hopeful."[14]

Mumford maintains an ambivalent position at

this point. He hopes for substantial resistance to what he regards as the fatal power drives of technocracy and yet he shares with others a high measure of skepticism—though Mumford's skepticism is rooted in a healthy appreciation for the fragile character of counter cultural movements throughout history. This long-range historical perspective can indeed serve to correct overly enthusiastic estimates of what the counter culture can do to redeem human frailty.

Counter Culture and the Despair of the Young

Those who would understand the inner dynamics of the counter culture must come to grips with the life experience of the young. They have lived through a very special history. Born in the Eisenhower years, nurtured in the hopes of the Kennedy years, reared in the frustrations of an endless war under Johnson and Nixon, the young have learned that hope is a rare and precious commodity. Their *despair* (manifest in the drug scene) and their *desperation* (manifest in acts of political terrorism) bespeak their condition of hopelessness *(de-spes)*. Out of the traumas of Chicago, Dallas, Memphis, and Los Angeles, they have raised their cry, a cry addressed to a people supposedly representing "Judeo-Christian" civilization. But did we hear their cry? Can the mass media or the corporate state hear such a cry? Do we not receive their anguish as an expression of nihilism rather than a passionate outcry for justice and compassion?

Many of us who marched with the hundreds of thousands in the Vietnam Moratorium of November, 1969, in Washington experienced this peculiar combination of despair and hope as we marched past the White House where the president sat cloistered with his TV, watching a football game. This largest gathering in the nation's history had come together to voice their dismay and their hope. The ritual chant of "Give Peace a Chance" led by Pete Seeger, with thousands of swaying fingers formed in V's, gave the event its own special liturgical significance. It was a day marred only by the distracting violence of the Weathermen at the Justice Department. But it was a day in which the president turned his back and the major television networks all but ignored the event, fearful perhaps of loosing the wrath of the vice-president.

The young now know that they have little to lose and much to gain in their break with the old culture. As Kurt Vonnegut's Billy Pilgrim expressed it, they have suffered their powerlessness over the past, present, and future. They have endured the major burden of the Vietnam war— a war justified and expanded under political administrations of liberal reform and sometimes managed by America's most distinguished business leaders and academicians. But they will not easily give in to this constricted, oppressive bind. Nor will they accept the narrow choices now open to them. They will no longer be content with the "lesser of two evils" doctrine of "Christian realism." They have no interest in a faith commitment that teaches them to exercise power "realistically" without questioning the character of the system wielding that power. They know with bitterness that the American people were betrayed in the presidential elections of 1964, when they thought they were making a significant choice between Johnson and Goldwater on the issue of war and peace.

This sense of betrayal and disenchantment with the direction of the American dream took on a special poignancy in the summer of 1969, when the United States sent two men to walk on the face of the moon. It was a stunning technological triumph. For a moment we were all proud Americans. Even Dr. Ralph Abernathy of S.C.L.C. was momentarily overcome with awe as he viewed the launch at Cape Kennedy—forgetting at the time that he had come to dramatize the incongruent lack of wealth and technology in the poverty programs. Most Americans seemed to think it was worth 40 billion dollars.

Then, a month later, in upstate New York, another kind of nation gathered in numbers over 400,000 to celebrate quite opposite values. With Arlo Guthrie, Joan Baez, Bob Dylan, Sly and the Family Stone, and a host of other folk-rock performers, the phenomenon known as "Woodstock Nation" emerged. In several days of rain and music, journalists marvelled at the spirit of the assembly, its capacity for order, kindliness, and festivity. Indeed, what other city of that size had ever gathered in such a euphoric mood?

Out of Woodstock, a rock group, The Credence Clearwater Revival, expressed something of the despair and hope of the new nation:

> Long as I remember,
> Rain's been comin' down,
> Clouds of mystery pourin',
> Confusion on the ground.
> Goodness through the ages,
> Tryin' to find the sun,
> And I wonder, still I wonder—
> *Who'll stop the rain?*
>
> I went down Virginia,
> Seeking shelter from the storm.
> Caught up in the fable,
> I watched the tower grow.
> Five year plans and New Deals,
> Wrapped in golden chains.
> And I wonder, still I wonder—
> *Who'll stop the rain?* [15]

This rock *kyrie eleison* cries for an end to the rain of death and deceit. Beyond bureaucratic reform it asks for a sign of hope. There is a widespread note of impatience and cynicism. Shortly after the 1970 elections I heard out the complaint of a bright undergraduate who had spent considerable energies on behalf of a liberal senatorial candidate in New England. He was one of many who had given himself to the "new New Politics," chastened by defeats at Chicago and angered by the American incursion into Cambodia. But he had his fill of reform politics. He had given it one last magnificent try, and his cause failed. A seasoned professor was seated next to us at dinner and quietly commented to the student, "You invest too much hope in politics. Politics cannot bring in the kingdom of God; it can only put off the advance of the kingdom of evil." The Niebuhrian in me rejoiced, but I knew immediately that this chastening word could not be heard by the student.

Adults committed to liberal democracy must expose themselves to the widespread feeling of political impotence and cynicism felt by large numbers of the young in America. This erosion of confidence has largely generated the movement towards alternate forms of cultural change. No one has better caught the depth of this disenchantment than Larry King:

College kids, especially, are not what they used to be. Presidents who lovingly speak of peace while aggressively waging war no longer fool them. Old fossils who vote to send them to die for corrupt Asian governments in the name of obscure freedoms, while closing their eyes to acts of genocide against Black Panthers are quickly recognized as frauds. Screwing is better than killing, to say nothing of being ever so much more moral, and the young know this where their fathers did not. Pot being no worse than alcohol, they know the insanity in an alcoholic judge's sending a pothead to jail on the word of a drinking prosecutor slowly murdering his own liver—while Washington subsidizes tobacco growers and cancer research from the same pocket. They know that Eisenhower lied about our U-2 spying missions, that LBJ lied about the Gulf of Tonkin and much to follow, that had the Pentagon told the truth all these years about its "kill ratios"—seven-to-one; ten-to-one; more—then the Vietcong would be more severely damaged than we now find it. They know the wide gap existing between the claims of institutional advertising and institutional performance, as is proved in malignant forms when they attempt to place Manhattan phone calls or when a black man can't secure a loan outside the lairs of loan sharks or when doorknobs fall off or basements leak in new $50,000 split-levels and when the rich architects of faulty automobiles assign private detectives to dig up dirt on Ralph Nader. They know that careless ecological crimes are committed by our industrial kings against the land they are supposed to inherit (provided they don't die in Asia, on the campus of their personal Kent State, or attending a Democratic National Convention) and that Dr. Billy Graham, the Nixon Administration's official moralist, has not provided leadership on a major social crisis in twenty years, if ever: let them eat platitudes. They know that John Wayne, Bob Hope, Mendel Rivers, and other patriots who most publicly proclaim the need for more efficient killing tools, and young men to enthusiastically employ them, have never served a military day in their comfortable, fat old lives. They know that J. Edgar Hoover is a despot, a tyrant, a vainglorious bureaucrat who runs his G-man corps with all the daily democracy attending a banana republic—and that not a man in Congress, or the White House, has guts enough to say so.[16]

It is over against this kind of feeling that the counter culture must be understood. Alienation and dissension have grown rampant as the promise of traditional institutions have shown signs of atrophy and corruption. Critics of the counter culture will fail in assessing the driving power of the disillusioned young unless they take full account of this failure of leadership. Then they can begin to comprehend the desperation that drives the Weathermen, the mad caravan of Ken Kesey and his "Merry Pranksters" across the West,[17] the disruptions of Jerry Rubin and the Chicago Seven at both the Democratic Convention and Judge Hoffman's courtroom, the mounting number of draft resistors. Madness is countered with madness; absurdity with absurdity. Lewis Mumford has suggested that all such desperate acts—however insane and nihilistic they appear to conventional moralists—do serve to awaken the human community to the sickness of our institutions and to disrupt those who blindly serve technocratic power. Needless to say, such understanding will be hard to come by, and many will continue to confuse the desperate reactions to the sickness of the old culture with the promise of the new. In every cultural transformation, there are iconoclastic "wreckers," and critics often find it convenient to merge iconoclasts and builders.

Implications for the Church

Hopefully, Christians will find it possible to make such a discriminating evaluation of the counter culture and to judge critically those who claim to speak out of a new vision. Christians should be able to confess cultural bankruptcy where they find it and to welcome those who explore new sources of human understanding and structures for justice. We must resist prematurely throwing up cultural blinders or accusations of theological heresy if we are to perceive what is underway. We must be sensitive to the fact that all builders of new creations move into an unformed, dark, and often chaotic situation. Answers, solutions, programs, and symbols will come out of great struggle and testing. We, above all, should remember that those who pursue a vision in faithful obedience will go out like Abraham, not knowing exactly where they are headed but clear in their search for a city with foundations.

We must also be open to the possibility that our time is a time of the mutation of human consciousness. We should know that cultures do experience morphological shifts. Our sense of what is real and where it is found has changed and will continue to change. We should remember too, that times of cultural transformation are times of religious creativity. The critical two centuries between the eighth and sixth centuries B.C. saw a dramatic change in human consciousness and religious understanding. In Greece, the power of human observation was greatly enhanced through sophisticated speculation. In Israel, the prophets Jeremiah and Isaiah called their people to an inward covenant exalting mercy over sacrifice. China gave birth to Lao-Tzu, the father of Taoism. India saw the writing of the Upanishads, in which the priority of devotion over ritual act was affirmed. And, in a far northeastern corner of Indian civilization, a Prince Gautama set out on a new path of human liberation.

The consequences of the cultural shift of those two centuries are to be found in new categories for understanding man's place in the world, his relationship to his fellow creatures, his language and art and religion. New vision meant new structures of human community. The old "functionalists," devoted to maintaining the system of the day, were replaced by the visionaries and voluntaries who undercut the old systems with the right questions and with life styles that enlarged the human experience.

Such historic mutations of consciousness threatened forms of religious life that could not discriminate between the originating sources of faith and the cultural forms in which they were expressed. While the Christian faith has always borrowed the cultural forms of the time, its most faithful theologians have known that a cultural gospel was a truncated and distorted gospel. Karl Barth was foremost in warning contemporary Christians that the purity of the gospel was to be found beyond cultural forms. During his visit to America, he reminded his audience that the object of the science of theology is not "a bird in the cage, but a bird on the wing."

The integrity of the Christian message is not necessarily jeopardized by cultural transformation. Indeed, we must be open to the possibility of reclaiming lost or neglected elements of Christian experience as the strength of a particular cultural system wanes and a counter culture appears on the horizon.

If in our encounter with the present signs of a counter culture in our midst, it appears that the movement represents a rejection of Western Christianity or a substitute for the church, we would do well to restrain ourselves from premature judgment. The encounter should lead us rather to reflection on our own history and the points at which the promise of the counter culture and the promise of the Christian gospel meet. We must resist the temptation to stop at all the usual barriers and gaps and contradictions. We must test out our traditional vocabularies and formulas and give much energy to systematic listening and imaginative speculation. In such a posture we may discern new possibilities for appropriating the faith handed down to us through the centuries, knowing that the sustaining power of it is forever shattering the forms we use to express it. Our experience with earlier "counter cultures" should give us confidence in the present encounter and insight into the promise it represents.

2

THE NEW
MYSTICISM

> It poured with rain the day I left. But I was filled
> with excitement, a strange exuberant sense of tak-
> ing wing. I didn't know where I was going, but I
> knew what I needed. I needed a new land, a new
> race, a new language; and, although I couldn't have
> put it into words then, I needed a new mystery.
>
> —John Fowles, *The Magus*

When thousands of American students gathered
together once more in May of 1970 to protest
the U.S. invasion of Cambodia, there was a strange
and curiously new element amid all the familiar
language of protest. On the White House Ellipse
in Washington were heard neither the usual slogans of American radicalism nor the evangelical
Christian rhetoric of earlier Washington protests.
Instead, loudspeakers carried the century-old
Sanskrit chant of Hindu and Buddhist tradition:
"Om, mani padme om" (literally, *"Om,* the jewel
is in the lotus, *om").* The mantric syllable *Om,*

chanted on this occasion by the poet of the beat generation, Allen Ginsberg, represented something other than the frantic and sometimes obscene gestures of such protest.

Here was one Western poet, initiating thousands of American youth into a chant promising peace and salvation—at a moment of their greatest despair. The jewel—timeless quiet and absolute clarity—was in the lotus—transient, caught in the death of time. For this moment, *nirvāna* could be glimpsed in *samsāra*, the illusory world of time and space, desire and anxiety. While the press did note the incongruity of this ritual chant at a protest rally, none of the reporters caught the significance of this ancient formula from the East ministering to the political despair of Western youth.

And yet, the Eastern mystic dimension was not that new to the American youth culture. They had read D. T. Suzuki and Alan Watts back in the fifties as the "identity crisis" dawned and Western disenchantment deepened. In the mid-fifties, the "silent generation" turned in its searching to the mystic innocence of J. D. Salinger's *Catcher in the Rye* and *Franny and Zooey*. Franny, one of the precocious children of that age, was fascinated by the ancient "Jesus prayer" ("Lord Jesus Christ, have mercy upon me") and the effect that a constant repetition of that prayer would have on the person praying. She saw the desired aim to be the same as that of the Nembutsu sects of Buddhism and the Hindus meditating on the *Om*:

> "You get to see God. Something happens in some absolutely nonphysical part of the heart—where the Hindus say that Atman resides, if you ever took any Religion—and you see God, that's all." She flicked her cigarette ash self-consciously, just missing the ashtray. She picked up the ash with her fingers and put it in. "And don't ask me who or what God is. I mean I don't even know if He exists." [1]

Such was the groping of the anxious adolescents of the post-war generation, going out not knowing where they were going but seeking a truth with foundations from the East.

And when the atomic age dawned early on July 16, 1945, an intensely intelligent young physicist, J. Robert Oppenheimer, against the blinding light of the desert at Los Alamos, remembered two lines from the *Bhagavad-Gita:*

> I am become death, the shatterer of worlds;
> Waiting that hour that ripens to their doom.

Nor was Oppenheimer the last troubled intellect of the West to find meaning in the mystic tradition of the East. Germany's Herman Hesse, England's T. S. Eliot, America's Thomas Merton —all enlarged the Western, Christian framework through the intuitive wisdom of the East.

45

Overcoming a Bias Against Mysticism

To really look at the mystic revival in our time, we must first come to terms with the deep bias in our thinking against most mystical tendencies. Surely for those over 30 the words "mystic" and "mystical" connote "escapism," "passivity," anti-historical movements, intellectual vagueness, possibly neurosis. It is an aversion easily come by and nourished by a long and sometime undistinguished tradition of kooks, fakirs, spiritualists, charlatans. The concept has been used to cover the shoddiest of feelings and the absence of rigorous thought.

Especially among the conventionally religious the aversion to "mystical" practice runs deep. Western religion manifests itself as a belief system, intellectually respectable and capable of being grasped by the mind of man. Protestant pastors over 30, educated under the prevailing neo-orthodoxy of Barth and Niebuhr, can examine for themselves the weight they give to words like "mystic," "vision," "contemplation." The "theology of the secular," emerging from Gogarten and the seminal clues of Bonhoeffer, shifted Protestant attention even further from the wisdom of the contemplative tradition.

Perhaps Bonhoeffer's phrase, "the world come of age," suggests what many feel has happened to the mystic dimension: it has been eroded in a world "mature" in scientific, causal thought. The mystery at the core has evaporated. Nature and space have been "conquered"; time has been mastered through space travel and drug technology; birth has become a biological fact, not a cosmic wonder; death is merely the end. Hemingway and Beckett have reported to us in their own way that the glory of death is no more —there is only the cold grave; the body is simply a piece of garbage that no longer "works." As one of the characters in Tom Stoppard's *Rosencrantz and Guildenstern Are Dead* says, "Being dead simply means that you aren't there any more." How unlike the perception of the Venerable Bede, probably the most learned man in Western Europe in the eighth century, who saw man's life like the flight of a bird out of darkness into a lighted room and then into the dark. The dark was still fraught with mystery, and one could still enter it in a trust that transcended simple fact.

Gabriel Marcel, more than most philosophers of our day, has waged a battle to maintain the limits of mystery in our world.[2] He argues that we have restricted our epistemology, our perception of the world's reality, to the "knowing" of the scientists. We too often have approached our world as a *problem* to be solved, in which all the "stuff" of reality is "out there" before us, capable of being touched and tested. Marcel reminds us that the world can also be approached as a *mystery*, which cannot be reduced to a problem capable of solution since all the evidence is not out there before us; but we are in it, and the only viable stance is one of *participation* and *communion*.

How ironic that physicists and microbiologists must remind Western man of this mystery at the core of life. How curious that a Teilhard de Chardin, grounded both in science and theology, should bring the word to the church that at the heart of the evolutionary process the divine mystery is present!

All this suggests how difficult it is for Western Christians to reappropriate the mystic dimensions of their own tradition and distinguish between occult magic and genuine mystic dimensions in the counter culture. We have been ill-equipped for the emergence of the new mysticism. Very few seminaries in the last three decades have seriously exposed their students either to the mystic tradition of the East as represented in Buddhist or Hindu culture, or, indeed, to the long mystic tradition of Western Christendom. How can we begin to do honest dialog with the new mysticism when we are unfamiliar with the experiences of Teresa, John of the Cross, Meister Eckhart, the mystic undercurrent in Luther,

Schweitzer's great study of Pauline mysticism? We are keepers of religious sanctuaries (some would say museums) where we maintain the tradition, the theology, the ethics that came out of the originating events of Nazareth, Jerusalem, and Tarsus—but we are strangers to the initiative events. We see no burning bushes. We sniff around the rims of extinct volcanoes, but no lava flows, no fire burns. We are strangers to the perceptions of Daniel and Ezekiel, the Revelation of St. John, and the visions of William Blake.

Perhaps the counter culture, with its strong visionary elements and its mystic longing for realities beyond the power of machines and technical reason, can initiate word-bound Protestants into the mysteries of a faith where bushes burn. Indeed, if we are to cut through all the unfortunate connotations that cloud the "mystic" vocabularies, let us simply come down to the Greek root, *myein*, "to initiate," "to close one's eyes." At that point, as a minimal concession, we at least can consider the possibility that other realities than those of the external world are possibilities before us. We can contemplate our very existence, our place in the flux of time, our relation to all living beings, our intimate links with nature, our creaturely limits, and a horizon against which new possibilities can be imagined and new resources marshalled. In such a stance, we can practice what the phenomenologists advocate: the suspension of all our given moral and intellectual categories and an openness to new images, new frameworks, new goals.

Again, this posture is not easy to come by in a world driven by speed, numbers, organization, rationality, compulsive power. Indeed, the contemplative life with its mystic dimension seems escapist and powerless. And so most of our churches as they gather for worship allow little or no time for quiet meditation. That is too risky. It may be simply what Paul Tillich called "holy emptiness," awkward, embarrassed silence. So we cover up these gaps in our liturgical actions with organ interludes and frame our silences with programs of confession or scriptural inspiration. We allow little room for the individual to seek his own depth, to come together with others in a silent, wordless affirmation. And then we are surprised when a Dag Hammarskjöld comes along and death reveals his contemplative life.

Toward Understanding the Mystic Experience

Where did we go wrong? How can we reclaim those elements of our faith that can minister authentically to a generation now turning either to Eastern traditions or the surrogate drug mysticism of Timothy Leary? Let us begin by reminding ourselves what we are looking for when we refer to "mysticism."

Since a serious study of mysticism is like entering a maze or walking over trembling quicksand, it may serve us to remember William James' attempt at understanding the mystical experience. In *The Varieties of Religious Experience* James identifies four marks of mystical experience:

1. *Ineffability:* The subject of it immediately says that it defies expression, that no adequate report of its contents can be given in words. It follows from this that its quality must be directly experienced; it cannot be imparted or transferred to others.

2. *Noetic quality:* Although so similar to states of feeling, mystical states seem to those who experience them to be also states of knowledge. They are states of insight into depths of truth unplumbed by the discursive intellect.

3. *Transciency:* Mystical states cannot be sustained for long. Except in rare instances, half an hour, or at most an hour or two, seems to be the limit beyond which they fade into the light of common day.

4. *Passivity:* Although the oncoming of mystical states may be facilitated by preliminary voluntary operations, as by fixing the attention, or going through certain bodily performances, or in other ways which manuals of mysticism prescribe; yet when the characteristic sort of consciousness once has set in, the mystic feels as if his own will were in abeyance, and indeed sometimes as if he were grasped and held by a superior power.[3]

With these marks as a beginning point, we can also use some kind of typology of mystical experiences, since the range includes everything from the trance states of Tantric Tibetan Buddhists to the holy quiet of Pennsylvania Quakers.

One of the best of current typologies is from the poet, W. H. Auden.[4] He suggests four distinct kinds of mystical experience:

> The Vision of Dame Kind
> The Vision of Eros
> The Vision of Agape
> The Vision of God

He makes it plain that the mystics are unanimous in saying that they do not see anything in the physical sense, although the first three kinds are concerned with a vision of visible creatures, quite often visions of extraordinary vividness. But the "seeing" and "hearing" of the mystics are, as St. Teresa affirmed, with "spiritual eyes and ears."

The Vision of Dame Kind, for Auden, is the experience of the non-human, natural world— although it could, by imagination, include the numinous significance of a city, for instance. In this category of experience, trees, oceans, mountains become numinous and charged with holiness. Distinctions between beauty and ugliness, utility and the unserviceable disappear. The self is "noughted" for the moment, absorbed in what Gerard Manley Hopkins called "the inscape of things." Wordsworth and Van Gogh clearly had this kind of vision.

The Vision of Eros is again a revelation of creaturely glory but it is focused on the glory of a single human being. It is more than lust or sexual infatuation; it is a passion that transforms the subject and brings an infusion of extraordinary psychic energy. "When in love, the soldier fights more bravely, the thinker thinks more clearly, the carpenter fashions with greater skill." [5] Plato, Dante, and Shakespeare have illumined the Vision of Eros and the church has puzzled over its own estimate of this evaluated human experience.[6] But it remains an experience which grasps lovers and opens to them a world of ecstasy and delight.

The Vision of Agape is a rarer type of experience and yet, without it, there would be no church. For the Christian, Pentecost is the prime example of an experience in which plurality, equality, and mutuality were present in a single community. We may see much the same expression inverted in the demonic possession of a group grasped by a collective hate or a collective sense of superiority. The Nazi rallies were the other side of Pentecost.

The young know something of this experience in their extended families, their communes, their drug culture communities where they get high "with a little help from their friends." The hunger for friendship, intimacy, belonging is crucial in the counter culture. Where all too often the church offers only a rationalized bureaucracy, the young seek a communal mystique and a sense of "family" most families no longer provide.

The Vision of God is even rarer. It is reserved, say the Gospels, for the "pure in heart." It was the end of man for the early Church Fathers. While the Old Testament cautioned against direct visions of God and indicated that we can expect only oblique glimpses of the back-side of deity, the hunger for "union," "identity," and communion continued as part of the early Christian community. While theistic mystics will always risk heresy in claiming anything like identity with the divine—remember Meister Eckhart in the 14th century and the Sufi Al-Ghazzali in the 11th—the movement towards an ultimate vision of the divine is important in all traditions. St. Paul's hymn of love in 1 Corinthians 13 echoes the same hope: "for now we see in a mirror dimly, but then face to face."

Again, the Vision of God is not an act of intellectual comprehension: "A God comprehended is no God" (Tersteegen). The Vision of God is marked off from worldly knowing:

> For all other creatures and their works, yea, and of the works of God's self, may a man through grace have fullhead of knowing, and well he can think of them: but of God Himself can no man think. And therefore I would leave all that thing I cannot think.

For why; He may well be loved, but not thought.
By love may He be gotten and holden; but by
thought never.[7]

Auden is careful to remind his readers that while all four kinds of mystical experiences are, in themselves, good and none contrary to Christian doctrine, all of them are at the same time dangerous:

If [the subject] allows himself either to regard the experience as a sign of superior merit, natural or supernatural, or to idolize it as something he cannot live without, then it can only lead him into darkness and destruction.[8]

Given this warning, what can we say of the unquestioned erosion of mystic sensibilities in the Protestant tradition? Has not the Reform tradition from the beginning ruled out the contemplative life as alien to the "justified" life through God's grace? Have not Protestants tended to regard contemplation as either quietism or "works righteousness"? Rudolf Otto's observation rings true: "For a Protestant to love mysticism is mere dillettantism: if he is in earnest, he must become a Catholic." [9]

Luther and Mysticism

And yet, the dominating influence of the mystic tradition cannot be erased completely from the Protestant tradition, as seen in Luther's life. During the critical years 1515-1518, Luther responded with enthusiasm to the practical mystic insight of John Tauler. By this time, the power of the great Dominican mystics—Eckhart, Tauler, and Henry Suso—had been checked by the trial of Eckhart for heresy in 1329, when Pope John XXII decreed seventeen of Eckhart's propositions to be heretical. Because of this atmosphere of suspicion, Tauler's was a more chastened and cautious mystic outlook.

Tauler was careful to stay within the prescribed boundaries of orthodoxy. Neither he nor Eckhart made autobiographical references to their personal mystic experience. There is an apocalyptic tone to much of his writing that reflects the civil and ecclesiastical strife of the 14th century. (This was also the time of "The Black Death.") But something important happened: the Dominican friars were asked to supervise the order and reform of convents, and as they preached and counseled these communities of educated women, Scholasticism lost its hard edge and a new contemplative tradition was nourished.

Luther was especially attracted to Tauler's emphasis on the uselessness of external works and his increasingly detached attitude toward Scholasticism.[10] Tauler did not stray far from the orthodox Thomist pattern: reason commands, the will obeys, emotions then fall in line. But once he had said that, he was inclined to follow the *Via Negativa* of pseudo-Dionysius and invite his hearers to enter "the wilderness," "the divine darkness" where "the wild beasts of your animal senses and forces reign supreme, into God's solitary, still and free ground." [11] In an Advent sermon, he exhorted his hearers to follow Jesus, "so that we may go out after Him into the wilderness of our own hearts, wherein God lies hidden to us." [12]

This mysticism of the dark marked the middle stage of Tauler's mystical discipline, following the initial stage of ecstasy and preceding the moment of union and the reduction of the natural self to nothingness. This cathartic movement into the darkness has been a mark of Western mysticism ever since Dionysius. Before new cultural creativity can erupt, the old lights, frameworks, and categories must be dimmed. In the primal dark, new images can be discerned. The King James Bible has an electric verse describing the approach of Moses to Sinai:

> And the people stood afar off, and Moses drew near to the thick darkness *where God was* (Exodus 20:21).

It is thus no wonder that young Luther, troubled by a rigid Scholasticism and the excesses of ecclesiastical corruption, found nourishment in the *Theologia Deutsch* of Tauler and commended it to his friends—after the Bible and Augustine! [13] To be sure, Luther rejected the substance of classic mystical teaching as alien to the gospel of Christ, especially "bridal" mysticism of union and the pseudo-Dionysian elements which he took to be a speculative by-passing of the incarnate Christ. He showed great regard, however, for the mystical teaching of Jean Gerson (1363-1429), the influential chancellor of the University of Paris, because of Gerson's clear portrayal of the mystical ascent *through* Christ rather than *to* the incarnate Christ.

Rudolf Otto, the great German scholar of the mystic experience, was not hesitant in placing Luther in the mystical tradition. He saw in Luther a form of mysticism that combined the element of fascination and awe with the bliss-giving character of a gracious God. Luther's mysticism contained, he argued, "the boisterous, almost Dionysiac, blissfulness of his experience of God." [14] But Luther, like St. Paul, followed a "Christ-mysticism" and not a "God-mysticism." And it is *faith* for Luther, rather than knowledge or love, that is the basis of the moments of "creature feeling" and union.

> So that when Luther says that faith makes man "one cake" *(ein Kuchen)* with God or Christ, or holds him "as a ring holds a jewel" *(sicut annulus gemmam)*, he is not speaking any more figuratively than when Tauler says the same thing of love. [15]

Harvard's church historian, George H. Williams, takes a more cautious view of Luther's mystic temperament. While agreeing that Luther's sense of childlike trust is very much like the classical *amor mysticus* and that the passivity of the will is marked in Luther's sermons, Williams sees mysticism functioning for Luther something like scaffolding, under which the prophetic dismantling of Scholasticism could occur and church reform could begin. The mystic teaching of Tauler, Gerson, and Eckhart no doubt shaped Luther's life and thought during this critical "bridge" period, but played no continuing role.

While the mysticism of the mature Luther may continue to be a matter of debate, there is little doubt that beyond Luther there is nothing quite like the mysticism of a Tauler or an Eckhart. In order for true mysticism to take root and flower, there would have to be a point of human receptivity. All mystic philosophy and psychology go back to Plotinus, the father of mysticism, and his notion of the "soul center" *(kentron* in biblical Greek), a sharp point, or apex. For Jerome, it was the *scintilla conscientiae;* for Tauler, *Gemut* or "root-will"; for some of the German mystics, the *apex mentis* or "creative reason"; for Teresa, the *centro del alma.*

As noted before, for Luther, this point became *faith* itself and any form of infused or acquired mysticism was suspect. Later Protestants lost all but a residue of mystical teaching. Despite the influence of the English mystics and especially the *Cloud of Unknowing,* the mystic tradition waned there after the 15th century. Some have claimed to find a mystic tendency in John Wesley, and it might be thought that Wesley's strong roots in the Anglican tradition of elevated reason and the influence of Gregory of Nyssa might be a sufficient basis for a restored mystic tradition. But Wesley was too much indebted to Lutheran justification and his own *via activa* to follow the *via contemplativa*. While very much inspired by William Law's devotional writing, Wesley had too high a sense of the church to follow the path of mystic withdrawal. He was horrified by the writings of Jacob Boehme with his God of the abyss, and he cautioned William Law against the perils of the mystic way:

> They who follow it need no Bible, no human teaching, no outward means whatever; being everyone able to stand alone, every one sufficient for himself! [16]

Such was the eclipse of the mystic tradition in Protestantism. One need only add the thunderings of Karl Barth against all mystic tendencies as examples of man's unbridled righteousness and his desire to build a "ladder to God." "The mystic's 'Way of Denial' is a blind alley, as are all 'ways.' The only way is the Way, and that Way is Christ." [17] Reinhold Niebuhr similarly concluded that all mysticism from Plotinus to the Eastern religious traditions represented a search for "an undifferentiated being," a being "bereft of all relationships and meanings." [18]

The Return of Mysticism

Now we find ourselves confronted with a mystic revival—a revival with many echoes of classical mysticism and yet with some distinctively new elements. The new mysticism is unashamedly syncretistic. It combines folk rock with straight gospel in the British rock opera, *Jesus Christ Superstar*. The citizens of the counter culture wear the peace symbol, the cross, the Egyptian *ankh* and the Chinese *Yang-Yin* in happy harmony. They find relief from drug addiction in the Sufi mystic, Meher Baba, and give themselves to the curious asceticism of the *Hare Krishna* group. A Zen monastery has been established in California, and the Sokagakkai movement of a Nichiren-Buddhist sect claimed 40,000 members in the Los Angeles area after eight years in this country. Clearly the missionary pattern has been reversed!

The Beatles went to India for instruction in meditation. The Maharishi Mahesh Yogi came to Harvard, and the young turn to the fantasy worlds of Tolkien and Herman Hesse. And at a time when some Christian theologians were grappling with "the death of God," a young rabbi explained why the young were turning to mysticism:

61

There are many indications of the renewed strength of mystical religion in our time. There may be some faddism involved in the interest in Zen Buddhism, for example, in the Western World since World War Two, but it is not all fad. Much of it has been a searching for new religious paths once it was understood that the God of traditional theism was dead and, as Paul Tillich said, deserved to die. In Judaism, there has been a revival of interest in Hasidism and Jewish mysticism, largely because of the writings of Martin Buber. Neither mysticism nor paganism requires a personal God: the God of both is the source out of which we have come and to which we must return. I believe that the time of the death of God will mean not only a renewal of paganism, it will also bring about a renewal of mysticism. My own deepest belief is that God is the holy nothingness, our source and our final home. Omnipotent nothingness is Lord of all creation. The old personal God of theism has been lost; the God of mystical religion will be renewed in the time of the death of God.[19]

What Rubenstein suggests is parallel to Luther's situation. Mysticism for Luther functioned as a bridge, as an interim scaffolding. It was a posture within which he could withdraw from the established culture and wrestle with new images of human understanding. In this sense, mysticism is a sign of cultural crisis, a return to primal being for roots, for fresh nourishment. It is a witness to an impoverished culture, a portent of revolt, and a hunger for new sources of wisdom.

Luther's crisis was both cultural and personal, and many in our time have found their own crisis in identity and vocation illumined by Luther's example as it has been probed by the psychoanalyst, Erik Erikson.[20] In their retreat from spent ideologies, the young have turned inward to seek another level of meaning. For the moment, they have opted for treading water in the mystic ocean and they are not about to accept rescue or safe lodging on a nearby isle. We may throw our traditional life preservers at them with good intentions, but there will be no faithful communication until those on the establishment side get their own feet wet in the mystic sea and remember Kierkegaard's notion that faith is learning to float over 70,000 fathoms of water.

The Mysticism of Herman Hesse

It is not possible here to survey all manifestations of mystic revival in the counter culture. An excellent report on the variety of these alternate stances to traditional Western religious values and institutions is to be found in Jacob Needleman's *The New Religions*.[21] However, it may be illuminating to examine the literary work of the German-Swiss novelist, Herman Hesse, since these writings have exercised an extraordinary influence over the generation in search of a counter culture.

Hesse's popularity in America has grown remarkably in the last ten years. In 1967, more than 100,000 copies of the short novel, *Siddartha,* sold within a year. In 1970, a 400,000 edition of *Nar-*

cissus and Goldmund, an allegory set in the Middle Ages, was offered for paperback sale. Clearly, for a generation turning from print to imagery, Hesse's writings were essential. He was the chief guru of the new mysticism.

Hesse (1877-1962) has attracted not only the following of the young. Rilke, T. S. Eliot, and Thomas Mann championed his work, and he received the Nobel Prize for literature in 1946. Mann found his *Steppenwolf* in no way inferior to Joyce's *Ulysses.* And yet, in the last decade, Hesse's place in German literary criticism has suffered considerably. He is not so widely read by the German youth, and many critics now regard his work as derivative, wrestling with shallow dualisms and over-simplified polar opposites. One critic has suggested that while American students are attempting to disengage themselves from a "materialistic environment with its worship of harsh facts to an essentially disembodied culture of the soul . . . "

> the German students in contrast are still busy shaking off the hangover into which their nation's recent indulgence in mysticism has plunged it. We may have touched here upon the fundamental difference separating the two cultures: For his countrymen Hesse represents the old metaphysical escapism, whereas on this side of the Atlantic he is a guide into the newly discovered ecstasies of the soul.[22]

There are good reasons why Hesse is so attractive to American youth. His writings are all directed at the young and about the problems of the young. He deals with the crises of school, of growing up, of choosing a vocation. Even when he writes about an older person, as in *Steppenwolf*, he is raising the question of a rebirth, a second adolescence. He elaborates the problem of the alienated, the outsider, the rebel against bourgeois values. And yet, like many American young, he displays a curious ambivalence towards bourgeois materialism and comfort.

The school and the state are the usual targets of Hesse's alienated characters. The school is viewed as a tool of the state, equipping functionaries for a rationalized bureaucracy. Nationalism, militarism, and aggressive industrialism are excoriated. Parental upbringing is faulted.

But protest and rebellion are not the whole of Hesse's message to the young. He has captured the frustration of a generation caught in the hold of one culture and yearning for the birth of another:

> Human life is reduced to real suffering, to hell, only when two ages, two cultures and religions overlap. A man of the Classical Age who had to live in medieval times would suffocate miserably just as a savage does in the midst of our civilization. Now there are times when a whole generation is caught in this way between two ages, two modes of life, with the consequence that it loses all power to understand itself and has no standard, no security, no simple acquiescence.[23]

In this no-man's land, Hesse has celebrated a new cult of experience. His youthful figures go out in search of sex, communion with nature, and inward visions. One of the earliest literary descriptions of a psychedelic "trip" is recorded in *Steppenwolf* as the alienated loner experiences a phantasmagoric realm of "the Magic Theater." And always, there is the yearning for the mystical vision. Steppenwolf "over the ruins of his life pursued its fleeting, fluttering significance, while he suffered its seeming madness, and . . . hoped in secret at the last turn of the labyrinth of Chaos for revelation and God's presence." [24]

There is much in Hesse that the American young have not bought. For instance, he maintains a stubborn reverence for history and tradition in all of his searchings, and he remains quite aware of his commitment to the secure and ordered world of the old culture. But the American young, unlike German youth, are not in reaction against mystical inwardness or metaphysics or Romanticism. On the contrary, they have responded with great enthusiasm to the German tendency to rebel against the word and reason, to accept what Hesse called "the matriarchal link with nature" in the German spirit: "We intellectuals . . . are all dreaming of a speech without words that utters the inexpressible and gives form to the formless." [25]

Something of the character of the new mysticism can be gleaned from three of Hesse's novels: *Siddartha* (1922), *Steppenwolf* (1927), and *The Glass Bead Game* (1942), sometimes titled *Magister Ludi*. All three are widely read and respected among the makers of the counter culture, and each suggests a distinct element in the new mysticism.

Siddartha was written after several trips to the Far East and is a short, romantic account of the life of a follower of the Buddha. Its eager reception by the American youth market in the late 1960s indicates something of the power of the Buddhist intuition over the young. Siddartha, a handsome young Brahmin, finds the comforts of home and wealth inadequate to soothe his restless heart and goes off in pursuit of salvation. After a period with an ascetic band, he learns that salvation is not to be found in rigorous ascetic practice nor in esoteric doctrines. He immerses himself in the world, learns the arts of love, becomes a wealthy apprentice to a merchant. He is borne a son by his lover and suffers the pains of alienation as his father before him. Finally, he returns to the contemplative life, disillusioned by the cycle of worldly suffering. He joins a ferryman and learns to listen to the voice of the river "which to them was not just water, but the voice of life, the voice of Being, of perpetual Becoming." [26]

67

By the river, he learns to wait in patience. There he "learns" the wisdom which could not be communicated through doctrine—the consciousness of the unity of all life. In the waters of the river, the voices of laughter merge with the voices of sorrow.

> They all belonged to each other: the lament of those who yearn, the laughter of the wise, the cry of indignation and groan of the crying. They were all interwoven and interlocked, entwined in a thousand ways. All the voices, all the goals, all the yearning, all the sorrows, all the pleasures, all the good and evil, all of them together was the world.[27]

In many ways this pilgrimage of Siddartha represents a spiritual movement quite contrary to what Western Christians would understand as the path to salvation. It is a negative movement, typical of Indian thought and intuition.[28] Moral virtues are stated negatively (e.g., *ahimsa,* non-violence). Salvation is not achieved through building up or adding something to the self, but through a process of stripping away illusions of selfhood. Many of the images of Christian salvation in the New Testament and elsewhere suggest a "building up," a maturing of the self, an enlargement, "the abundant life," growth toward "perfection," while Buddhist "salvation" and enlightenment come through the path of negation. The self is "awakened" and liberated not through commitment to a goal as in Calvin, but through suspension of teleology. There is no "plan of salvation," only *nirvāna,* only *sunyatā* (voidness). Thus, Siddartha ends his pilgrimage knowing that "seeking means: to have a goal; but finding means: to be free, to be receptive, to have no goal." [29]

What Calvin achieved through the doctrine of election and predestination, the Buddhists achieve through the negative movement of salvation—the destruction of self-conscious questioning of one's "spiritual" state. And the young have seized this posture of salvation with much passion. To be "saved" means to "drop out," to "let go," to dissolve the framework and order of Western thought and to experience pure Being. The root meaning of *nirvāna* is "to extinguish"—for the Buddha, to extinguish the root cause of suffering in desire. The consequence of this is described as a "cooling, soothing balm." Something related is expressed in the language of the counter culture when an experience which has shattered the usual framework of meaning is said to have "blown your mind."

Hesse's *Steppenwolf,* probably the most widely read of his books among the adherents of the counter culture, suggests quite a different mystical turn. Steppenwolf, an aging loner, alienated from respectable society, does not seek salvation in withdrawal and contemplation. He considers suicide, becomes a Dostoevskian "underground" man —a man plunging into Dionysian revolt, the raw energy of American jazz, drug-induced fantasies, and violent imaginings.

Healing and wholeness for Steppenwolf are not to be found in a return to nature:

> No, back to nature is a false track that leads nowhere but to suffering and despair. Harry can never turn back again and become wholly wolf, and could he do so he would find that even the wolf is not of primeval simplicity, but already a creature of manifold complexity. . . . The way to innocence, to the uncreated and to God leads on, not back, not back to the wolf or to the child, but ever further into sin, ever deeper into human life.[30]

Peace for Steppenwolf comes through absorbing more and more of the world into his soul and, at the same time, through separating himself from worldly limits and "painful individuation." It is again the path of the Buddha: "Reunion with God means the expansion of the soul until it is able once more to embrace the All."

While the classical Buddhist teaching does not allow for a doctrine of God (the ultimate is *sunyatā*, voidness), the Buddha did teach the negation of self, and Hesse's *Steppenwolf* sees this as central to the healing of human divisions. The divisions of "wolf" and "man," "flesh" and "spirit" are illusive simplifications. While man may find himself a single entity as a body, Hesse affirms that as a soul man has no simple unity. So Hesse lays bare in this novel of the underground hero "the fiction of the ego" and reminds his readers that Indian literature is free of this illusion: "The heroes of the epics of India are not individuals, but whole reels of individualities in a series of incarnations." [31]

This classical Buddhist doctrine of *anatta* ("not-self," *an-ātman* in Sanskrit) illumines Steppenwolf's path of salvation until at the end he learns to laugh with Mozart at the absurd, comic character of human life. Enlightened through a drug "trip," he comes to understand the illusion of personality in a way similar to that of a Buddhist: "Man is an onion made up of a hundred integuments, a texture made up of many threads." [32]

It is unfortunate that Hesse's *The Glass Bead Game* (or *Magister Ludi*) has not received the same wide reading by the young as *Siddartha* and *Steppenwolf,* for it represents his most mature work. It was for this work that he received the Nobel prize in 1946. In this story of Joseph Knecht's movement through a pilgrimage of worldly detachment and intellectual syntheses is found a significant turning point in Hesse's thought. The search for spiritual health, for contemplative vision is now yoked to the historical order and compassionate responsibility. As Theodore Ziolkowski notes in his foreword to *The Glass Bead Game:*

> It is possible to read *Siddartha* as a self-centered pursuit of nirvana, but Joseph Knecht gives up his life out of a sense of commitment to a fellow human

being. It is possible to see in *Steppenwolf* a heady glorification of hip or even hippie culture, but Joseph Knecht shows that the only true culture is that which responds to the social requirements of the times. *The Glass Bead Game,* finally, makes it clear that Hesse advocates thoughtful commitment over self-indulgent solipsism, responsible action over mindless revolt.[33]

The mystical dimension remains, but it is always set within and against the burdens of history. Hesse continues his search for peace and serenity but acknowledges that "there are those among us who are too easily satisfied, who enjoy a sham serenity." [34] Hesse now affirms the "cheerfulness" of the ascetics in the face of historical responsibility:

Such cheerfulness is neither frivolity nor complacency; it is supreme insight and love, affirmation of all reality, alertness on the brink of all depths and abysses.[35]

He acknowledges the pressures of history that led to the establishment of the "order" of Castalia:

A tremendous craving for truth and justice arose, for reason, for evercoming chaos. This vacuum at the end of a violent era concerned only with superficial things, this sharp universal hunger for a new beginning and the restoration of order, gave rise to our Castalia.[36]

But finally, Joseph Knecht (German for "servant") resigns the highest post of the order of Castalia and announces his desire to return to the larger world as a schoolmaster. It was too rarefied an atmosphere, too much a "bloodless" game in the history of ideas, lacking the "incomprehensible truth, reality and uniqueness of events." [37] Hesse understood the cultural imperative of renewal in an age of decay, and he put his finger on the critical educational task if a viable counter culture was to be established:

> Teachers are more essential than anything else, men who can give the young the ability to judge and distinguish, who serve them as examples of honoring the truth, obedience to the things of the spirit, respect for language.[38]

This mature vision of Hesse indicates something of the promise of the new mysticism—if Hesse's pilgrimage is followed by his young American readers. A culture worthy of replacing the old may indeed come, if through the labyrinthine way of self-centered isolation and Dionysian revolt the way might be found to equip a new generation with the insight and determination to build anew. Surely Hesse himself has suggested some of the resources that will nourish the new values and structures of community in the counter culture.

Christians and the New Mysticism

Christians who find themselves caught up in this age between the ages and often confused by the absence of mystic insight in their own tradition need not separate themselves from Western

Christendom in order to find nourishment for their hungers. They need not be completely empty-handed in their withdrawal from dead structures and traditions.

Among the major theologians of the post-war period Paul Tillich stood almost alone as one who revered the mystical dimension of his tradition and personally bemoaned the disposition of both Barthian and Kantian-Ritschlian schools of theology to decry the abuses of the mystical approach without affirming the salutary function of mysticism. Tillich's theology of the Protestant Principle included an appreciation for the function of mysticism to point us to "the abysmal character of the ground of being and to reject the demonic identification of anything finite with that which transcends everything finite." [39] Tillich knew the ease with which the substance of a sacramental and priestly tradition could be distorted and the media of revelation could be made substitutes for the revelation itself. "Even the final revelation needs the corrective of mysticism in order to transcend its own finite symbols." [40]

In the last volume of his *Systematic Theology*, Tillich struggled with the question of the compatibility of mysticism in Protestant theology and he left those who would encounter the new mysticism with some liberating clues:

There is no faith (only belief) without the Spirit's grasping the personal center of him who is in the state of faith, and this is a mystical experience, an experience of the presence of the infinite in the finite. . . . But the mystical experience is not identical with faith. In faith the elements of courage and risk are actual, whereas in the mystical experience these elements, which presuppose the cleavage between subject and object, are left behind. The question is not whether faith and mysticism contradict each other; they do not. The real question is whether the transcending of the split of subject and object is a possibility in man's existential situation. The answer is that it is a reality in every encounter with the divine ground of being but within the limits of human finitude and estrangement — fragmentary, anticipatory and threatened by the ambiguities of religion.[41]

I hope that the builders of the counter culture, in their quest for mystic insight, will look beyond the present limits of Protestant imagination and discover the full range of the Christian tradition: the strong emphasis on the meeting of human and divine will in Clement and Ignatius and Irenaeus; the purging strength of St. John of the Cross and the author of *The Cloud of Unknowing;* the bold grounding of the 14th century Dominicans, Suso, Tauler, and Eckhart. Then, perhaps, the agents of cultural renewal will lead Christians into a re-appropriation of faith as a vision—a vision in which bushes do indeed burn and the contemplative life feeds the life of moral action.

3

THE NEW
CONSCIOUSNESS

> To be capable of everything and do justice to every-
> thing, one certainly does not need less spiritual force
> and elan and warmth but more. What you call pas-
> sion is not spiritual force, but friction between the
> soul and the outside world. Where passion domi-
> nates, that does not signify the presence of greater
> desire and ambition, but rather the misdirection of
> these qualities toward an isolated and false goal,
> with a consequent tension and sultriness in the at-
> mosphere. Those who direct the maximum force of
> their desires toward the center, toward true being,
> toward perfection, seem quieter than the passionate
> souls because the flame of their fervor cannot always
> be seen. . . . But I assure you, they are nevertheless
> burning with subdued fires.
>
> —Herman Hesse, *The Glass Bead Game*

Hesse's words provide an appropriate text against
which one can question the reality of our present
cultural crisis and the possibility of a dawning
new consciousness. In the last decade in America,
we have experienced rather sharply the difference
between passion and spiritual force. Our political,

ideological, and theological passions are nearly spent; our activist ardor has cooled. Too many of yesterday's radicals are today's burnt-out cases. The old forms now only painfully remind us that they once channeled meaning and purpose and hope.

So we live as Hesse suggests, in an atmosphere of "tension and sultriness," uncertain as to whether we are witnessing the still smoldering fires of the old creation or the newly-generated fires of the new. While we hope desperately for fresh and enlarged perceptions of our situation, we remain cautious lest we give our passion and desire to "an isolated and false goal."

Such is the historical bind of the youth culture and, indeed, all who are concerned about the cultural possibilities of this bind. We have been reminded each day by the media of the growing alienation of the young from standard goals, professions, and institutions of our culture. Most of those who have "dropped out" have "tuned in" and "turned on" to a world of contrary realities: drug and natural mysticism, extended families, a preference for visual images over linear print, a rejection of hierarchical organizations for horizontal communities, and a rediscovery of the centrality of the body.

The young face their world with quite different sensory and cognitive equipment than the generation of the 1940s and 1950s. Television, the pill, space exploration, drugs, political frustration, and too much death have shaped for them a horizon of perception quite "counter" to that of most persons teaching and preaching and legislating in the established culture. Any high school or university counselor knows at least the symptoms of this crisis in the form of draft resistance, drug use, the heightened sense of vocational uncertainty, the break down of *in loco parentis* regulations, the decline in job applications for corporate positions, and the rise in the number going into community medicine, legal services, and ecological mobilization.

Charles Reich has sensed the larger significance of this shift in youthful perception and suggested through his use of Consciousness III an alternative to the technological society with its radically circumscribed consciousness:

> We can end or modify the age of science and we can abandon the Protestant ethic. In this sense, it has been a long, long time since we made any real choices; since the end of the Middle Ages, technology and the market have made our choices for us. Perhaps the culture just now being developed by the new generation—the new emphasis on imagination, the senses, community, and the self—is the first real choice made by any Western people since the end of the Middle Ages.[1]

While this note of hope will strike some Christians as a fatal brand of Romantic optimism, it should not becloud the fact that the severity of our cultural crisis does indeed portend such a fateful choice. Without that kind of openness to a new culture, Christians would never have formed their own community; and they must take care to examine themselves in such a moment and ask whether they are defending a cultural shell or standing within a faith open to cultural transformation.

Clearly, Reich sees Christianity as having failed as a source of human renewal. Like many intelligent critics, he sees Christianity asking men to "give up power, aggression and materialism for a promise of something better in another world, a world after death." [2] Reich argues for a change *now* that will initiate a new world of satisfactions and freedom. While Reich may quickly acknowledge that Yale's Chaplain, William Sloane Coffin, represents a distinctive, hopeful Christian voice, he knows, as do many of the young, that the Christian message is frightfully obscured by the baptism of technocratic culture by Billy Graham and the difficulty of separating authentic Christian witness from a web of idolatrous cultural commitments. The pain of this cultural admixture was most recently illustrated in the retreat of the Protestant Council of the City of New York from its decision to present Bob Hope with its "Family of Man" award for his "massive" contribution to humanity. At the last moment, under lively pressure from a group of younger ministers, the council gave a posthumous award to Whitney Young of the Urban League. Even so, the situation exposes serious deficiencies in the Christian leadership of America's largest urban area: an award was about to be made to a man who has made no public commitments on the critical issues of poverty, war, or racial justice and has gone to some lengths to gloss over dissent related to America's Vietnam policy. In the end, the Council retreated by honoring an "establishment" reformer, Whitney Young, rather than a churchman with clearer counter-cultural commitments, such as Jesse Jackson, Andrew Young, or Ralph Abernathy.

This unhappy wedding of Christianity and technocratic values should be faced by Christians before they engage in facile strictures against Reich and other advocates of the counter culture. It is all too easy to judge the Romantic elements of Reich as an illusive return to Adamic innocence, reunion with nature, and the development of a free and spontaneous life style. All of that *is* present and we should not be unmindful of the perils of Romanticism. However, we cannot escape the repressive situation which breeds a romantic yearning for freedom, community, and mystery by entrenching our life in a dying culture. As

Sir Kenneth Clark reminded us in his television lectures on *Civilisation,* despite the lack of a tragic vision, the Romantics *did* "defy all those forces that threaten to impair our humanity: lies, tanks, tear-gas, ideologies, opinion polls, mechanization, planners, computer—the whole lot." [3]

A hiatus has been reached in our time in which a movement towards a counter culture sees Western, Christian humanism to be a spent shell, a dead end for cultural renewal. The counter culture itself is viewed by the cultural establishment as an illusive hope nurturing a false consciousness, devoid of historical understanding, and too much governed by adolescent rebellion and love of chaos. There are few who have learned how to negotiate the boundary between these two cultures, and the communication across the gap is burdened by the differences of contrary states of consciousness and language. Reich counsels the followers of the counter culture with an irenic and nonchalant wisdom that reflects something of the Chinese philosophy of *wu-wei* (non-activity), which is deceptively shrewd in both the art of ju-jitsu (making use of the opponent's strength) and culture building:

> The plan, the program, the grand strategy, is this: resist the State, when you must; avoid it, when you can; but listen to music, dance, seek out nature, laugh, be happy, be beautiful, help others whenever you can, work for them as best you can, take them

> .in, the old and the bitter as well as the young, live
> fully in each moment, love and cherish each other,
> love and cherish yourselves, stay together.[4]

Christians should have no difficulty recalling similar counsel to those who came together in the first century under the repressive policies of an older imperialism. Parallel themes in the pastoral epistles and the Revelation of St. John also cherish a visionary hope over against apocalyptic expectations and the nurture of *agape* over against a provisional-critical relation to all "authorities." These early Christians could sympathize with the adherents of the counter culture and would find themselves more at home than in the rationalized and bureaucratized forms of a Christianity identified with the goals of technocracy: organization, production, number, efficiency.

Cultural Decay and Creation

If Christians are to separate themselves from an uncritical stance towards the old culture and a closed-critical stance towards the possibility of a new culture, they will need to give serious attention to the process of cultural formation. Cultures, constituting the whole range of language, values, social institutions and ideologies, depend for their continued existence upon an inner consciousness to enliven and sustain the cultural system. Cultures die when the consciousness of those within the culture no longer perceives sustaining realities.

Lewis Mumford, a longtime student of the history of cultural decay and regeneration, argues that there is a critical interplay in the process of cultural creation, a double and complementary movement: "materialization" and "etherialization." In the materialization movement pre-conscious activities such as dreams, intuitions, and incommunicable private experiences get "materialized" in words, art forms, persons. After their expression, a cultural milieu is shaped through the process of "etherialization," in which the newly incarnate truths are put into symbols, word formulas, and coherent world views. The time will come when the symbols and formulas of a particular culture lose their cogency and power to sustain creative life. All that remains is the lifeless shell, rituals without emotive power, symbols without ontological grounding.

Looking at our own history through such an understanding, Mumford is aware of the surprises waiting around every historic corner. He wonders over the motley band of counter culture Christians turning around the ideological and power system of the Roman Empire under Augustus. Who would have expected the law and order and weaponry of that "megamachine" to be so chastened by the emergence of the Christian community?

This fragile possibility could *not* have made it, and Mumford senses the same possibility today with regard to the "materialization" process of the counter culture:

The yearning for a primitive counter-culture, defying the rigidly organized and depersonalized forms of Western civilization, began to float into the Western mind in the original expressions of Romanticism among the intellectual classes. That desire to return to a more primeval state took a folksy if less articulate form, in the elemental rhythms of jazz, more than a century ago. What made this idea suddenly erupt again, with almost volcanic power, into Western society was its incarnation in the Beatles. It was not just the sudden success of the Beatles' musical records that indicated that a profound change was taking place in the minds of the young; it was their new personality, as expressed in their long, neo-medieval haircut, their unabashed sentimentality, their nonchalant posture, and their dreamlike spontaneity that opened up for the post-nuclear generation the possibility of an immediate escape from megatechnic society. In the Beatles all their repressions, and all their resentments of repressions were released: by hairdo, costume, ritual, and song, all changes depending upon purely personal choice, the new counter-ideas that bound the younger generation together were at once clarified and magnified. Impulses that were still too dumbly felt for words, spread like wildfire through incarnation and imitation.[5]

The new impulses and the current hunger for a new age presents an opportunity in which the Christian community can extricate itself from the pervasive culture and renew its life through encounter with new forms of human consciousness. The first steps involve, as Mumford suggests, the path of withdrawal and contemplation:

> Each one of us, as long as life stirs in him, may play a part in extricating himself from the power system by asserting his primacy as a person in quiet acts of mental or physical withdrawal—in gestures of nonconformity, in abstentions, restrictions, inhibitions, which will liberate him from the domination of the pentagon of power.[6]

As we have long known, this withdrawal will be costly and filled with great personal risk. It involves all the ambiguities faced by Martin Luther King, Cesar Chavez, and the Berrigan brothers. It involves exposure to the depths of our cultural abyss and abandoning the comfortable categories of the Western tradition. It demands a serious openness to quite alien ways of thinking about selfhood, community, and historic responsibility. It may mean that we confess the barrenness of our theological cupboards and the paucity of imaginative resources with which to face the shaping of a new culture.

Resources for Christian Renewal:
A New Consciousness

Religion has always been associated with a special state of consciousness as a means of viewing the world and perceiving the real. Through faith and ritual, man has found both distance from his world and a sense of unity with it. As man emerged from a primitive state immersed in a world of myth and magic which guaranteed an extraordinary sense of unity, he increasingly experienced himself as an isolated individual, moving against other selves and communities, experiencing contradictory myths and rituals. The evolution of human consciousness has meant the heightened experience of our selves as separate, discrete, and isolated beings. Religion sometimes ameliorated this isolation through its vision of an omniscient and omnipotent God, sometimes accentuated this separation by assuming a profound dualism between "this world" and "the beyond."

The most ancient religious formulas of Christianity were severely jeopardized in the formation of modern self-consciousness, especially under the influence of Descartes (1596-1650). For it was Descartes who reduced the self to the "knower" and reality to the reach of the mind. Both God and the external world, according to Cartesian thought, evolved out of the knowing self, the Alpha and the Omega. It was a precise and ordered philosophy, and it shaped the way generations of Western Christians came to perceive reality. Everything began and ended with the self, characterized largely as the cognitive self, the self divorced from feeling and imagination and will.

Much of the promise and energy of the counter culture involves a rejection of the Cartesian formula and a quest for a new consciousness. However, large numbers of Christians find themselves more or less caught up in Cartesian consciousness when they try to encounter the drug phenomenon, Eastern mysticism, the commune movement, or the ecologist's affirmation of man's deep roots in nature. We are "hung-up" on an inadequate basis of consciousness. We are rightly judged by Alan Watts (a former Episcopal priest who is widely read by the young for his books on "consciousness expansion" drawing on Eastern mysticism and psychotherapy) for our incapacity to see our world whole. He has often observed the threat of the contemplative life to the Protestant spirit and noted the ways in which liberal forms of Protestantism are influenced "by the mythology of the world of objects, and of man as the separate ego." [7] This Protestant man finds it difficult to give himself to pleasure and play, to imagination and mystery. He moves through his life pursued by guilt rather than pulled by hope. He has forgotten the critical distinction of Augustine between the things which are to be used and the things which are to be enjoyed.

Persons in such a state of consciousness will find it hard either to appreciate the values of the counter culture *or* the kingdom of God (they are not synonymous!). They will not be able to make the critical "turn" that initiates the new age. ("Unless you turn and become like children you will never enter the kingdom of heaven" Matthew 18:3.) They will be like the hearers of Jesus in the marketplace: "We piped to you, and you did not dance; we wailed and you did not mourn" (Matthew 11:17). Incapable of either play or tragedy, such people are locked into a world of limited range, separated from the larger human drama of renewal.

How can Christians begin to extricate themselves from such "false consciousness"? How can we penetrate the Cartesian consciousness that sees man as isolated "in his own subjective awareness . . . a detached observer cut off from everything else in a kind of impenetrable alienated and luminous bubble which contains all reality in the form of purely subjective experience"? [8] Are there clues for Christians in their own tradition that will enable them to participate resourcefully in the shaping of an alternative to a technocratic culture?

The answer will be found only in an arena larger than the Protestant world or even the total breadth of the Christian tradition. It will finally be claimed by those who join persons of diverse traditions in wrestling with the central issues raised by the counter culture and who can transcend cultural provincialism. Such a Christian was the late Thomas Merton, monk of Gethsemane Abbey. Merton pursued in his last years the possibility of a new Christian consciousness and the recovery of a life of contemplation—"contemplation" here understood not as a quest for some esoteric knowledge or experience, but as a necessary and special way of participating in the process of incarnation and redemption. Better than most, Merton sensed the spiritual vacuum occasioned by the cultural crisis and the imperative of freeing the Christian people from cultural bondage lest the faith become "an opiate of the people."

He did not expect all Christians to be contemplatives removed from the field of action. He *did* fervently plead that Christians not separate themselves from the contemplative orientation:

> Without contemplation and interior prayer the Church cannot fulfill her mission to transform and save mankind. Without contemplation, she will be reduced to being the servant of cynical and worldly powers, no matter how hard her faithful may protest that they are fighting for the Kingdom of God.[9]

Merton articulated the dead ends of a contemplative tradition based on the assumption that the empirical ego is the starting point of any spiritual growth:

> This state of affairs can never be remedied by the empirical ego's merely going through gestures of

purification and concentration, suppressing thought, creating a void in itself, sinking into its own essential purity, and so on. This is only another way of affirming itself as an independent, autonomous possessor now of thought, now of no-thought; now of science, now of contemplation; now of ideas, now of emptiness.[10]

Merton had both the grace and sense to realize that this was "bogus mysticism" at its best, schizophrenia, at its worst. He learned much from his studies of Zen Buddhism and pointed to a critical point in the Chinese development of Zen when Hui Neng, a master of the 7th century, rejected the cultivation of "emptiness" to attain *prajñā* (the intuitive wisdom of Buddhist faith). This master made sport of such contemplation as "mirror polishing," a pattern reflected in much Western contemplative tradition. Rather than sitting in studied silence to empty "the mind" of distracting images, Hui Neng instead focused on pure being or awareness as the prior, enveloping reality. "Mirror wiping" was seen as useless—because there was no mirror (self, mind, ego). Merton saw the importance of the Buddhist insight—that the experience of the Absolute means the loss of self —not as a denial of the self's existence, but as a radical question as to the self's priority in the process of salvation. The common element of both Buddhist and Christian "enlightenment" for Merton was that the flooding of light threw the self into darkness, noughting the self. It does not mean that the way of contemplation means the denial of flesh, sense, and worldly vision; it means that the beginning of real vision entails "the dark night of sense" in which insight is a beatitude.

This encounter with both Zen masters and Christian mystics led Merton to rethink traditional formulas of Christian contemplation and ask whether Martin Buber's "I—Thou" formula was the only way of establishing Christian consciousness—the theistic formula of God as an "object" of personal knowledge and devotion on the part of a clearly defined individual. Could we not learn, he suggested, from the noughting of the self in mystic experience and the *a priori* intuition of being in both Buddhist and Christian tradition?

Merton's Three Options

In his last writings, Merton posed the alternative forms of consciousness available to contemporary Christians. They are not "stages," but quite distinctive ways of seeing reality from the perspective of faith. These options throw much light on the present bind of Christians caught between changing cultures. The choices are as follows:

1. *Persisting in Cartesian Consciousness.* This is to continue the cultivation of personal self-awareness as a subject among and over against

other objects—including God. People exist in these "bubbles" of selfhood as detached observers, as the center of the only real universe. This kind of consciousness attempted to reach God as an object by starting with the thinking self—and made inevitable the so-called "death of God," according to Merton. God as mere object, an abstract concept bolstered by sheer effort of will, is unthinkable.

A host of Christians have awakened in recent years to find themselves in this camp and are fast moving out. They have no enthusiasm for maintaining this objective "God" of their ancestors, a deity strangely susceptible to cultural manipulation. They know it is a strained and unconvincing performance. They yearn to break out of this false consciousness and "do in" this "God" they know in truth is not the Ground and End of their life but a fiction of the thinking-self.

Some break out of this camp by proclaiming "the death of God" but remain restless without an ultimate horizon of meaning. Others will work with heightened Protestant zeal for "fellowship," "encounter," "openness," or "dialog," without depth. Some will try to smother the remnants of Cartesian consciousness in sensitivity training groups and immersion in sensory experience. Thus, Descartes' *cogito, ergo sum* is replaced by Esalen's *sentio, ergo sum*. Somehow, through in-

tensity of feeling, through sensation and movement, the self must be validated lest it perish. For
some, this liberation of consciousness will be
found in drug experience. Marijuana or LSD
becomes the *deus ex machina* that heightens self
awareness (consciousness "expansion") while the
user sees no other way of ecstatic expression ("getting out of myself").

2. *Shaping a New Ontological Consciousness.*
This choice raises the possibility of rethinking
the classical metaphysical position wherein one
begins not from the thinking, self-aware subject
but from Being (or Spirit, the Ground, the Void).
One does not think from one's self to a God-object
or world-object but begins with the intuition of a
field of being beyond and prior to the subject-
object split. This consciousness of Being is radically different from the Cartesian mode of consciousness. It begins with a network of relationship and interdependency; it is without the split
of the thinking, willing self and the external, dependent world and deity.

> The consciousness of Being (whether considered
> positively or negatively and apophatically as in Bud-
> dhism) is an immediate experience that transcends
> experience. It is not "consciousness of" but pure
> consciousness, in which the subject as such disap-
> pears.[11]

This position meets several movements in the

same direction out of the counter culture. It removes a heavy burden of self-consciousness by assuming that the experiencing self is posterior to this experience of the Ground, hence, as in both Christian and Buddhist mysticism, this "self" is neither final nor absolute but provisional and relative. The "self" has meaning only insofar as it is centered not in itself but "from God" and "for others." This stance acknowledges the fragile character of selfhood and its fullest realization as it is "dissolved" in ecstasy, wonder, self-giving abandon, and its center in "the still point of the turning world." God is the center of the great chain of being and interdependency: "the one centre of all, which is 'everywhere and nowhere,' in whom all are encountered, from whom all proceed. Thus from the very start this consciousness is disposed to encounter 'the other' with whom it is already united anyway 'in God.' " [12]

The reality of God is thus not a matter of cognition but intuition and participation (communion) in an infinite ground of openness and relationship —"indeed of a kind of ontological openness and an infinite generosity which communicates itself to everything that is" (in nature and history). This openness of the generosity of Being is not something to be acquired through belief, "but a radical gift that has been lost and must be recovered (though still in principle "there" in the roots of our created being)." [13] Once more, there is the reminder of mystical roots long neglected in which a human center was affirmed, a center that linked the creature with Creator and Creation. A host of names were used: *apex mentis, Funke der Seele* or *scintilla conscientiae* (Eckhart), *kentron* (Plotinus), *Gemut* or *Seelengrund* (Tauler), the *centro del alma* (Teresa of Avila). All such terms were ways of expressing the deep hunger of the human spirit for transcendence and ultimate grounding.

Merton realized the problems inherent in re-appropriating this classical Christian tradition extending from Anselm to Paul Tillich. He knew the difficulties of conceiving of God as either Immanence or Transcendence and the need to state in non-metaphysical language the reality of God as "grace" and "presence." Despite the problems of metaphysical language, Merton saw the continuing vitality of this ontological consciousness and its universal role in the religious traditions of East and West as a ground out of which loving action can be sustained.

3. *Following a Biblical, "Missional" Consciousness.* Merton called this "the new Christian consciousness," though it was clearly not his own point of departure and a position that he considered troubling and inadequate. This stance tends

to reject "Hellenic," "metaphysical," and "mystical" categories. The experience of Being Itself as an ontological ground through intuition is viewed a near impossibility, for "being" is seen as an abstraction, a strictly logical cipher. It is not a matter of existential experience.

This is not to say that the "new Christian consciousness" is a return to Cartesian consciousness. Rather, it is a chastened form of individual consciousness, what Merton called "reflexive ego-awareness." For some, it would be a consciousness shaped by phenomenologists such as Husserl and Merleau-Ponty. It affirms the primary datum of human experience as the ultimate test of truth and sees self-awareness as blocking the possibility of the intuition of Being. The focus of such consciousness is outward to history, events, and political and ethical goals.

At points, this consciousness *may* be viewed as parallel to biblical, eschatological consciousness with great emphasis upon prophetic judgment and historic responsibility, but at many points it appears to abandon the full tension of primitive Christian consciousness. Paul Tillich often cautioned against the easing of this tension between the "religious obligation" (the activist, horizontal element) and the "religious reservation" (the mystical, vertical element). It may well be that a Protestant theology of the Word, calling people to missionary engagement, has exhausted itself in a horizontal drive toward immediate social-political goals and left many without an ultimate ground of hope.

This anti-metaphysical, anti-mystical consciousness more and more separates itself from the question of God's presence in the creation and places the locus of authority in God's "Word" as a summon to mission. The divine reality is not an experienced transcendent ground which reduces all else into insignificance (including the self-aware subject) but the inscrutable Word calling us into community for mission. Such a consciousness, present in the "acoustical" and missional theology of Barth and Bonhoeffer, has governed much recent Protestant theology and ecclesiology. God is not "seen" or "intuited"; he is "heard" as a summons to action; for some, he is "where the action is." While this consciousness has enabled the Christian community to mobilize itself for social action beyond the concerns of individual piety, it has not nurtured communities with an integrity beyond that of persons committed to provisional social goals. As Merton noted: " . . . the rather more fluid idea of community which 'happens' when people are brought together by God's word may perhaps remain very vague and subjective itself. It may conceivably degenerate into mere conviviality or the temporary agreement of political partisans." [14]

There is extensive evidence in both church and counter culture to support Merton's fears of a community without ultimate grounding. The ranks of tired liberals, battle-fatigued radicals, and polarized congregations witness to the precarious character of Christian community in a time of cultural change. Our immediate loyalties divide us—class, race, generational and sexual identities—and we are left without an ultimate sense of belonging to one another, under a common judgment and blessed with a common hope.

Merton's three options are helpful guides to rethinking Christian consciousness against the promise of the counter culture. They indicate something of the limits and inhibitions of our openness to new forms of perceiving reality. The pace of social change, the breakdown of established communities, and the expansion of transcultural exchange of ideas has left many of us bewildered and paralyzed. Parents cannot understand their children, and older church leaders puzzle over the actions of younger clergy. Polarized groups operate on quite contrary perceptions of what is real and where it is located. Our liturgies, our theologies, our ethics have hardly begun to absorb the impact of a new consciousness striving to create a new culture.

Toward a New Christian Consciousness

The shape of the new Christian consciousness in America is still in the formative stage. Again, we should be reminded that we are a relatively "young" tradition capable of adaptation. We know we must move beyond the forms of consciousness appropriate to European Christian culture. We know we must move beyond the secure categories of Barth and Tillich and embrace a larger network of meaning. The breakup of the old sources of cultural sustenance has been a long time coming. In 1931 Karl Jaspers boldly sketched out the dimensions of our bind and announced that we had reached a point of no return. He knew that history had driven us out of unreal forms of consciousness and that "although the possibilities of an expansion of life have become immeasurable, we feel ourselves to be in so narrow a strait that our existential possibility is deprived of its breadth." [15] It is this sense of constriction that has generated the counter culture to seek a consciousness open to new sources of personal nurture. Jaspers anticipated the ennui of the reformers, the temptation to tranquilize ourselves in self-forgetful pleasures or the peaceful return to nature. But he acknowledged these to be dead ends:

One day iron reality would again confront him and paralyse him. For the individual, thrust back into

99

his own nudity, the only option today is to make a fresh start in conjunction with the other individuals with whom he can enter into loyal alliance.[16]

Such is the alliance of the counter culture: held together in rejecting obsolete forms of consciousness; united by their determination to see the world anew.

Unfortunately, too many Christians do not share with the counter culture the sense of "the ripeness of our time." "Iron reality" has yet to force them out of their cultural securities and expose their nudity. That is why mainstream Christians nurtured in the theology of the West and tutored under neo-orthodox "realism," can learn much at this juncture from the cloistered Thomas Merton, the monk separated from the world, yet a man who knew the strength of the contemplative tradition and the healing power of the dark night of the soul. It is not easy for Protestants to listen to such cloistered wisdom. We have so long prided ourselves on our capacity to move in worldly circles that we are severely threatened by the spiritual discipline represented by a monk given to meditation and interior prayer.

Yet we desperately need a recovery of something like the contemplative tradition if we are to separate authentic faith from its cultural shell and discover those interior and transcendent sources of renewal that are the promise and goal of the

100

counter culture. We know only our hunger. We have yet to purge ourselves of cultural idols and narrowness of vision and we scarcely believe the promise of the gospel that beyond our cultural despair and paralysis there is a wide space of freedom and grace.

St. Gregory of Nyssa (c. 330-c. 394), a theologian of the mystical life, saw God as present to man as he revealed Himself to Moses, first in light, then in the cloud, and ultimately in the dark. He took as his prime clue for the riddle of the future a line from Paul: " . . . one thing I do, forgetting what lies behind and straining forward to what lies ahead, I press on toward the goal for the prize of the upward call of God in Christ Jesus." [17] Gregory's clue was in the posture of *epekstasis,* "straining forward." It was a gesture of trust, a movement into an uncertain future, a willingness to abandon everything in order to quench his thirst for a larger vision.

Something like Gregory's posture of *epekstasis* will serve both Christians and makers of the counter culture as they shake loose from forms of false consciousness and throw themselves into the future—honest about their unfulfilled hungers and willing to learn the difference between mere passion and spiritual force.

101

4

THE NEW COMMUNITIES

> Tradition has been broken, yet there is no new
> standard to affirm. Culture becomes eclectic, sensa-
> tional, or phony. (Our present culture is all three.)
> A successful revolution establishes a new commu-
> nity.
>
> —Paul Goodman, *Growing Up Absurd*

The old communities in America—the family,
government, church, university—suffer from the
atrophy of cultural degeneration. The values that
once sustained them have suffered the pains of
urbanism, with its loss of primary human relationships, and mass technology. The car, television, drugs, contraceptive pills, an economy
with no work for the young, a divisive war, new
cultural idioms in music and art and literature—
all these have fragmented the traditional groupings. Communal life in America has taken a sharp
turn from the time of William Whyte's *The
Organization Man* (1956) to Mike Nichols' film,

The Graduate (1967). American religious life has made the same shift from the suburban, middle-class evangelism of the 1950s (Norman Vincent Peale, Billy Graham, Peter Marshall) to the "movement" type ministries of the 1960s (Martin Luther King, Father James Groppi, William Sloane Coffin).

Exodus from the Old Communities

There is much truth in Theodore Roszak's observation that the present movement of the counter culture is more of a flight *from* decadence than a movement *toward* any single new pattern. It means thousands of young Americans fleeing from their comfortable suburban homes to adopt the life of a gypsy or a circus performer or a fugitive. Like Benjamin in *The Graduate,* they have said no to the plastic culture of affluent suburbia, and they have set out on a quest for a new communal style, driven by a need to satisfy a qualitative hunger in a quantitative milieu. Benjamin is educated in the Ivy League, blessed with a California home, endowed with wealth and fun items such as a sports car and scuba diving equipment. Yet he hungers for identity, relation, passion, and a viable future.

Benjamin is not alone. His name is legion in the new communities of the counter culture. As Kenneth Keniston observed in his study, *The Young*

103

Radicals, the alienated student dissidents are largely children of professional, liberal, middle-upper-class parents.[1] While most come from warm and permissive families, others seek surrogate families beyond the nuclear unit. This latter group knows the deficiencies of a strong family unit and looks among their peers for familial support and friendship. Having been reared before television screens that mirror our broken domesticity *(Julia, Here's Lucy, My Three Sons, The Courtship of Eddie's Father, Family Affair),* the young have found their communal life in the new communities: communes, rock groups and festivals, runaway centers for teenagers, meditation centers, underground churches, organic farms, collectives formed around special tasks (educational reform, political re-distribution of power, or community organization).

But even more important than the flight from a plastic suburban culture and the internal deficiencies of the nuclear family, the counter culture has formed new communities to kindle and maintain the flame of the new consciousness. The young separate themselves into distinct groupings because they are attuned to vibrations most of their parents cannot or do not sense. They are "alienated" by their special insights, perceptions, and commitments; they are into a political and mystical vision that exalts solidarity, communion, "participatory democracy." Emerging from the recovery of existential anxiety in the 1950s, the students today know that they live in a communal vacuum and that the established forms of community fail to offer adequate answers. The impetus behind the formation of Students for a Democratic Society went beyond the radical, anarchist ideology with which SDS is so often tagged in the press. The Port Huron Statement of 1962 was a humane manifesto, struggling to avoid platitudes and slogans and attempting to set forth the hunger of the young for a more inclusive and responsive community:

> Loneliness, estrangement, isolation describe the vast distance between man and man today. These dominant tendencies cannot be overcome by better personal management, nor by improved gadgets, but only when a love of man overcomes the idolatrous worship of things by man.[1]

SDS was but one of many groupings among the young for getting themselves "together." As chonicled earlier, the young have experienced a long history of abortive reform and compromised revolutions: the new industrialism, the New Deal, the Great Society, the urban revolution, progressive education, reform in the churches—all producing change but not community. Harvard's late Dean of Divinity, Samuel H. Miller, frequently described this failure of the modern age by saying that our presentday communities were like bags of marbles: we touch only at the edges of our lives; we live in great collectivities, but we hunger for community.

So the young have largely divorced themselves from traditional circles lest the impulses they experienced be smothered by technocratic togetherness. Sometimes it seems little more than a huddled sense of protection against the impersonal world of corporate bureaucracy. At other times, there are glimpses of a new vision of what human community might be as fed by the new consciousness: a community that rejects the notion that man is an empirical ego, that we must follow the myth of objective consciousness and allow the "experts" to dominate our lives, that man is to ignore his roots in nature and neglect the vision of faith.

The Character of the New Communities

Again and again, during the period of "confrontation" between the established institutions and counter culture forces—whether the institutions were churches, universities, or units of government—what was most often asked was for these institutions to become responsive communities. Blacks asked for community control of their schools; students in Berkeley asked for a "People's Park"; students all over asked for a role in university governance. They asked churches about their corporate investment portfolios (with regard to South Africa, General Motors policy, Black Reparations); they asked universities about their encroachment on the neighboring communities (Columbia's gym and the University of Chicago's relation to Woodlawn). One exasperated university administrator once cried out: "What do these kids want? For the university to be the church?" Well, yes, it does appear that something like that is desired by the young. They have observed sociologists at a university like Chicago studying and sampling Woodlawn for more than a decade and they want to see analysis linked to moral vision and responsible action. They have heard the church talk about reconciliation, but they doubt our commitment when reconciliation means costly grace.

The consequence of this realization is something like an inversion of the values of 19th century America: rugged individualism, the unquestioned exploitation of nature for profit and industrial expansion, a simplistic morality, the Protestant work ethic. This value system, which sustained the conquest of the American continent and the development of the corporate state, fails now to meet the new values of the young. Their attack begins with what Roszak has described as an assault on the "most precious work in our vocabulary": the word "I". The counter culture, both through mystical religion and the drug experience, challenges "the reality of the ego as an isolable, purely cerebral unit of identity." [2] As seen in the appeal of Herman Hesse and Buddhist intuition, the young have responded to those sources which express the dissolution of the isolated ego and offer solidarity, the mystique of communion, interdependency with the whole of reality. The interdependency sought clearly counters the interdependency of technological organization which restricts freedom and encourages competition.

Drugs, rock music, dress and mystical religion may all be viewed as means the young have used to separate themselves from oppressive treatment on the part of technocratic managers. It is a way of opting out and declaring one's independence from the machine and the prison of the ego. In effecting this reversal of destructive individualism, they have turned to the Orient for insight into new models of community. They have now largely rejected the "conflict models" that are represented in the Western political and religious tradition. It is a tradition that extends from Zoroaster to Karl Marx and operates on the assumption of a struggle between opposing forces: darkness and light, good and evil, matter and spirit, proletariat and bourgeosie, male and female. In such a model, clear cut moral distinctions are possible and the language of polarity tends to sublimate reality. Guided by these lights, we in the West knew what was "divine" and what was "human," what was "masculine" and what was "feminine"; we knew that both politics and religion were about conquests and conversion.

The young people have turned to another model, a model of complementary and related opposites. It is expressed in the symbol out of China, the *yang* and *yin,* a symbol now as evident among the young as the cross or the fish in the early Christian gatherings. In this symbol—a circle separated by double curves—the principle of unity and the interpenetration of opposites is affirmed. The opposites give and receive of the dark and light. There is a small dark circle on the light side; a small light circle on the dark side. Neither side is complete without the other. *Masculine* and *feminine, good* and *evil, divine* and *human* are not separable categories. Reality is deceptively perceived through conflict models that fail to account for this mixture and complementary character. In the Christian tradition, something of the same principle was expressed in the phrase of Nicolas of Cusa (1401-1464), *coincidentia oppositorum,* the coincidence of opposites, through which hierarchical principles of grades and levels of reality were rejected and transcended.

Thus, the new communities of the counter culture are deeply suspicious of groupings formed on the basis of strict ideological lines or divisions and qualifications based upon sex (or even age, if their elders share in the new consciousness). They have painfully experienced the fragility of communities generated in opposition, dependent for their survival on moral scapegoats and the "true believer" mentality. They have seen too many cadres of mere opposition mount the barricades of protest, only to dissolve when the tear gas clears away. Likewise, they have learned something of the evanescent quality of communities formed around drug experience and dependencies. Like Woodstock and *Alice's Restaurant,* the good feeling and unity of delight soon dissolves, and intimacy needs a more substantial bond.

No wonder, then, that the counter culture has turned to a wide range of models in its search for authentic and enduring community. It has made use of the experience of the Israeli *kibbutzim,* the Diggers, the Levellers, a variety of Christian sects, the roving Buddhist monks, the nomadic American Indians. Some appropriate the African tradition of the extended family. Charles Reich makes a great deal of this recovery of "tribal" life and the "circle of affection" that binds those engaged in the work and play of an extended family. He recalls the unity of peasants in a medieval

110

guild or of craftsmen engaged in the building of a cathedral and regrets that the technological age allows no such an integral linkage of manual work and creativity in a communal project.

The anarchistic, utopian elements involved in this return to primitive cultural models aim for a drastic scaling down of the size of human groupings so that a maximum of intimacy, comradeship, and shared work are possible. The intention in such a decentralized, small scale tribal or village community is to allow for human diversity and frailty rather than expecting larger and more centralized units to deprive the primary unit of facing its own problems and possibilities. In many ways, the cry of the counter culture makers for "participatory democracy" and "power to the people" is very much akin to the cry of the state's righters and opponents of a centralized federal power, though both are subject to some of the same drawbacks: isolation from the needs of weaker elements in a larger community and a tendency to become parochial and defensive about internal weaknesses.

Something can be learned about the character of the new communities by remembering the classical elaboration of Max Weber (as based on a distinction of Tönnies), which illuminated the meaning of community *(Gemeinschaft)* as distinct from "association" *(Gesellschaft).*[3] While the "associational" world operates on the basis of a functional use of persons towards productive goals and builds on the conflict of interests, the "communal" world looks for relationships within which love and unity of purpose override conflict. This is not to say that the communal world eschews conflict. It welcomes conflict but deals with it under a prior understanding of the basis of that particular community: a covenant, a set of commitments, tasks to be done. Within the context of this commitment to the community, conflict and disagreement serve only to test the seriousness of the commitment.

The young see groupings that have conceived themselves as "communities" operating as if they were "associations." They see both the church and the university violating a personalistic ethos by forms of governance that are more hierarchical than democratic. They know the sure and terrible ways in which the "Peter Principle" (by which the incompetent are elevated) works with a vengeance in both school and parish to rob students and parishioners of personal care. They know that we tend to rule more by edict than consensus and have created a vast mythology to cover our failure to provide an open and responsive community which can absorb honest criticism in love and laughter—and change.

When they are judged against the stable and mature communities of Western culture, the new communities do appear fleeting and sometimes comical creations. Their disorganization and unbridled dissent makes one wonder if they will ever survive. And yet they keep together largely because they do not worry overmuch about their organization or institutional survival. Rather they give themselves to celebrations marked by Dionysian abandon, childlike innocence (kite-flying, flower-picking, skinny-dipping), and participation in natural and communal "happenings."

They have also shown inventiveness in developing alternate structures for human learning. In virtually every university center in America, "free universities," "experimental colleges," and "dissenting academies" have arisen. They offer noncredit courses and seminars on everything from exotic cookery to Zen meditation and Marcusean analysis. They wrestle with the issues of the counter culture, the dead ends of the old culture, and diversions that will entertain them for the interim period. Very often the universities in the area will respond to these alternate models by restructuring the curriculum to include seminars on similar issues, by providing coed dormitories and an atmosphere where the teachers can assume a role of advocacy rather than the stance of academic objectivity.

In and around university centers, the residential

communes proliferate. They are composed mostly of students but also of faculty and other adults who band together on the basis of professional concerns, artistic vocations, or community service. Some are together because of a commitment to political radicalism; others are a strictly laissez faire community of painters, potters, and leather workers, who move in and out of this "family" during their stay in the university.

In an increasing number of situations, the new communities are beginning to focus on modest and realizable goals for alternate ways of effecting political reform. They have detached themselves from grandiose schemes of dismantling the "system" and are thinking along the lines of achieving "community control" or establishing new "liberated zones" in new communes or abandoned towns. For the present, at least, they are trying to find the means to co-exist within the corporate state through the support of those trying to realize a new life style.

Berkeley is one sign of hope that such liberated zones can be realized and be tolerated by the surrounding "straight" world. The young there have undergone long years of frustration in trying to create an alternate culture. Political defeats through encounters with the police and Governor Reagan over the "People's Park" issue, demonstrations over the war and the Free Speech

Movement, and harassment from the police over a host of issues—all have generated the determination to gain for Berkeley indigenous institutions and community services related to the new counter culture. Apartments in the area have taken out the separating back fences where communal gardens now grow (vegetarian diets and organic products are a popular feature of the young). Over 4,000 people have joined the "Berkeley Food Conspiracy," a cooperative food market featuring organically grown products. There is a medical service, a free university, a rotating emergency committee (sort of a police force) working on a 24-hour basis, a labor gift plan— providing a listing of skills in the community to be exchanged free of charge. There is a studied concern over the presence of transients and freeloaders who sweep through Berkeley mainly in the summer and sponge off the generosity of the Berkeley citizens. The coalition there has moved cautiously in the direction of political contests and has fought for a referendum granting Berkeley community control of the police under a separate administration from the neighboring suburban communities.

There are similar movements in Boulder, Colorado; Madison, Wisconsin; Fayetteville, North Carolina; Cambridge, Massachusetts; and wherever significant numbers of young people gather.

The lines between the two cultures are drawn in dramatic and sometimes oppressive ways as mayors and police officials learn for themselves of the gap between the generations. While the young are attempting to work out some internal cohesion for the new culture—including a legitimate work style, political strategies, and ritual style—they must also learn to negotiate with politicians under pressure from an aroused citizenry over drug abuse, the violation of housing codes, and crimes related to the maintenance of costly drug habits. Too often, as in Haight-Ashbury, these youth ghettos become a site for "freak watching" by tourists or vulnerable to exploitation by outside gangs. Boston, Atlanta, Boulder, and Chicago have all faced such situations. In some, the politicians have exercised wise restraint and learned to tolerate a parallel form of governance from within the new communities.

The growth and maturity of the new communities has been seriously inhibited by the widespread hostility and misunderstanding of the youth culture in America. The campus disturbances, civil disobedience, the challenge to the norms of both national and religious traditions—all have served to heighten the barriers toward understanding the humane forces behind the search of the young for viable and life-serving communities. The young, who only two decades ago were condemned by the mass media for their caution and silence and resignation to lives of secure mediocrity, are now pilloried for breaking with established society and forming their own environment, their own cultural language and art, their own ethic and religious vision.

The consequence is that middle America tends to locate unrest on the campuses or in hippie communes rather than in the Pentagon, the FBI, or a host of corporate offices where the exploitation of our environment is accepted. Again and again the young have found themselves caricatured by the establishment. As one student put it: "It's like the people in the subway who draw beards on the ladies on the poster. We're made into something we're not!" While the new communities spread through the land, the old communities do not yet seem prepared to understand the dynamics behind them.

Thus far, the Christian people in America have not mobilized the resources that are peculiarly theirs in critically and sympathetically evaluating the counter culture. While many churches have opened coffee houses, teenage runaway centers, and drug rehabilitation centers, and have embraced some of the new music in their worship, we have generally tried to absorb the youth culture within the old culture. We have tried the way of tokenism and sometimes corny faddism in trying to "be with it." Like Billy Graham at the rock festival in Florida with glued-on sideburns and dark glasses, we have become cultural voyeurs in the circles of the young. We will attempt to co-opt their styles and understand their communities, but we draw back at the point of identifying with their consciousness—for that means a drastic re-orientation on our part.

The Church as Perceived by the Young

Among the institutions bypassed by the young in their search for new forms of community are the mainstream American churches. They are generally perceived as being irrelevant agents of a religious bureaucracy without either prophetic commitment or a communal mystique. They are seen as nourishing a private piety unrelated to the corporate sickness of our social structures. While leaders of the student movements will acknowledge the helpful presence of the church during the civil rights crisis and the passage of the nuclear test ban treaty, they see the church as almost totally culture-bound when it comes to the tragedy of the Vietnam war.

The intention here is not to raise the expectation that every pastor should model his ministry on Father Groppi or Bill Coffin in identifying with dissident students or third world communities.

That would be too facile a judgment. What *is* suggested with even more devastating implications is that the church is too often unrelated to the critical breaks in our society to even pray about them! I have observed a Southern community in the throes of racial anguish and violence —and seen the mainstream churches go on with their fund raising campaigns and never even acknowledge in their prayers of intercession that their neighbors were suffering under a dual system of justice. We thus find ourselves alienated from those who do feel the tears of the social fabric, who do question the legitimacy of established institutions, and consequently we are immersed deeper and deeper into a blessing of the cultural establishment that is far removed from Augustine's discriminating vision of the "two cities."

That is the prophetic failure of the church. There is also the mystical, pastoral failure. Let me again draw on a personal experience involving the tragic death of four students in a sailing trip. Some of their friends in the same residential college wanted to attend the funerals in the home town churches. They did so, and found at the first funeral that the service was given over to a local funeral home replete with plastic flowers and plastic smiles. The death of their friend was not dealt with, nor was there an attempt to speak meaningfully of the Christian hope.

Stunned by this churchly treatment of their friend, the students returned with the idea of holding a joint memorial service around an ancient poplar tree at the heart of our campus. At dusk on an October evening, they invited the parents and girl friends of the dead students to join them. They had created a great circle of glowing light by placing candles in grocery sacks. They had wired up a stereo to play recordings by Simon and Garfunkel, the Beatles, and Judy Collins. They invited me, as a campus pastor, to participate (not to "lead"). I read a poem by Dylan Thomas and offered a short prayer. Then roommates, teachers, and friends stood and spoke. They recalled critical and joyful moments with each of the students—their struggles with the draft, their opposition to the war, their political hopes and frustrations. Readings were given from Herman Hesse, John Donne, the Beatles, and letters from the students. Their religious questions were raised and affirmations voiced. At the end a gangling reporter from the university newspaper stood with hands in his pockets, looked up at the night sky and uttered a heartfelt, passionate prayer. Then we all stood for a bit, greeted the parents, wept, thanked one another, and gradually departed.

Not one of us left that glowing circle that evening without knowing that we had been for a small time in a rare and genuine form of human community. We all stood united before the ultimate mystery of death and sensed something of a numinous power enabling us to bear our grief. We had participated in holy ministrations, honest communal acts that had met our sorrow and sustained us in a diverse but substantial faith. That community would probably never gather again, but it offered something the students did not find in the church.

To say this is to acknowledge the rarity of such occasions when community does occur. With countless experiments in liturgical innovation— folk masses, jazz liturgies, dialog sermons, dance and touch and drama—we *still* must confess that we have nothing unless we have a semblance of real community where peoples' lives do meet at the center and not the edges of their existence. What is too often observed by the young is a forced style of togetherness in which critical differences are glossed over for the sake of "harmony" or "fellowship," and there is something like a gentleman's agreement not to penetrate beneath that happy exterior to the depths of anguish and need—where real faith might come alive.

Finally, the young seem especially sensitive to

the fact that the church has taken on many of the characteristics of the culture and, rather than serving as a formative force to transform cultural patterns, it is the mirror image of the culture. This judgment is based on the way the church is organized (with boards after the corporate image), funded (with a blend of New Testament and Madison Avenue), and mobilized for action (into "programs" more often than ministries). They view our church buildings and observe how closely the pastor's office conforms to a business office, and they wonder about all the space given to worship on one day a week, when space is needed for a host of community service needs. In some extreme cases, they will observe areas designed for worship in which the most prominent features are not imaginative symbols of faith, but heating outlets, organ pipes—or the pulpit wherein the preacher holds forth (the church's equivalent of the technocratic expert). There are even churches where the Cartesian consciousness is manifest in the most direct way—such as each member of the congregation sitting in his separate, canvas director's chair (the epitome of liberal Protestant consciousness).

This tainted image of the church as a mirror of technocratic culture can be corrected only through the imaginative and deliberate efforts of Christians nourished by a transcendent vision.

The body of Christ must be delivered from narrow cultural gospels and parochial visions. It must exercise critical discrimination in examining the sources that feed the counter culture and learn to identify with those elements integral to the Christian faith.

Sources of Renewal for the Christian Community

Christians familiar with the first 300 years of their history as a new people within the Roman Empire should immediately mark their kinship with the cultural underground. Visionary and powerless, they too lived with the uncertain task of sustaining a revolutionary hope in an alien environment. The pastoral letters of Peter and John, along with the Revelation of St. John, bear out this kinship: "We know that we are of God, and the whole world is in the power of the evil one" (1 John 5:19); " . . . according to his promise we wait for new heavens and a new earth in which righteousness dwells" (2 Peter 3:13); "Behold, I have set before you an open door, which no one is able to shut; I know that you have but little power, and yet you have kept my word . . . " (Revelation 3:8). The church needs to learn from the counter culture that the door really is open for cultural reconstruction. And the task will be

—for both church and counter culture—to negotiate that entryway with as little paranoia and Manichaean delusion as possible. In following the lead of the counter culture, the church can lay hold of its own tradition in a fresh way. Let me indicate at least three such points of possibility.

The Necessity of Cultural Detachment: Our most recent history and theology have led us to believe that worldly withdrawal, contemplation, and mystic vision were escape routes from Christian responsibility. We have proceeded either on the basis of "Christian realism" or "religionless Christianity" to learn operative skills in power politics or confused the role of theology with sociology. And we find ourselves surprised and puzzled by a generation turning to religious styles that cut across the grain of post-war Protestant theology.

We have forgotten the dynamic of the underground church. We have missed the point behind the monastic orders and the renewal that came out of their counter cultural movement in the Middle Ages. We have not thoughtfully considered the models offered by the example of the Moravian brethren *(Unitas Fratrum)* who, in the 18th century, found themselves oppressed in Moravia and found refuge in Saxony at the hands of Count Zinzendorf, where they created a new style of congregational life and gave impetus to the missionary activity of the entire Protestant tradition.

There were also the Quakers (with their tradition of mystic quiet, the inner light and a courageous witness to the peaceable kingdom), the Shakers (with their joyous celebrations of music and dance, their emphasis on male and female principles in the deity), the Mennonites (who broke with the established state church in Switzerland and stressed the apostolic tradition of nonresistance). All of these strands represent Christian movements that are counter cultural in their determination to witness to realities beyond present cultural norms. They were cultural subversives. But they were not paranoid or Manichaean because they lived out of the transcendent power of the kingdom of God beyond the fears and inhibitions of cultural exclusion.

This contemplative detachment can be recovered by the church as it has been recovered in the counter culture. The church can shake off its cultural dependencies and become once more a formative force in culture building—light, life, yeast, and salt. But if it cannot learn to detach itself, its qualifying power will be lost. "If salt has lost its taste, how shall it be restored? It is no longer good for anything except to be thrown out and trodden under foot by men" (Matthew 5:13). The gospel of Christ is viewed by many in the counter culture as a message the church cannot embrace without separating itself from national ideologies and cultural binds. They see us equivocating before the demand to "repent" and failing to ground ourselves in the reality of the kingdom of God.

From a Gospel of Forgiveness to a Gospel of Liberation: The counter culture can also assist the church in turning its efforts and understanding toward future possibilities rather than just offering forgiveness for past sins. Too often the message of forgiveness and justification has meant cultural resignation, a low horizon of expectation, and an emphasis on reform efforts at improving the system without questioning the direction and validity of the system. To rethink the gospel in terms of the counter culture is to move beyond justification to sanctification, to move beyond forgiveness for the past towards hope for the future. It is to recover the New Testament understanding that while forgiveness is necessary throughout the Christian life, it is always a beginning point and not a resting place. Repentance and faith for both Jesus and Paul mean orientation toward the future. Our mission is the same one announced by Jesus: release, sight, liberation.

Those who proclaim the ingression of the new, however, are most often outside the walls of the church. Those who preach the gospel of liberation are quite frequently those branded by the culture as "hippies" and "peaceniks." When it comes down to the desperation of the young for signs of hope, it is usually not the church who sings "Let the Sunshine In." This prophetic and mystic tradition has passed over to new forces of liberation. We should not, however, automatically assign an aura of sanctity to the counter culture. The promise of human liberation is the hope of both church and counter culture, and both will continue to run the double risk of antinomianism (liberation as license) and cultural complacency (salvation as a resting place).

Two sterling examples of the church risking a gospel of liberation are the congregations of Judson Memorial Church in Greenwich Village and Glide Memorial Church in San Francisco. These parishes, set in the East and West capitals of the counter culture, have shown the imagination and will to effectively relate the gospel to human liberation. These congregations lean into the future and try to test through direct encounter the viability of the coalitions representing a new consciousness: the Black militants, the sexual liberationists (female and gay), the legal defense groups, the ecologists, the mystics, the political utopians. These congregations have exposed themselves to the weakest points of our culture. They know the cry of the young and the poor and the colored for justice in a land where dual systems prevail. They know the agony and depression of spirit that go with the pursuit of new human possibilities. But they also know the appropriateness of the church being in the business of liberation, and they point the way for others to search out their mission as a broker and advocate for groups and coalitions who are about the same business. They know also that politics and sociology are not the only routes to cultural transformation; they have daringly challenged the icons of the old culture by a ministry of film, drama, and creative arts. These efforts are always controversial and sometimes "mind-blowing"—which again suggests the relation of the new art (especially rock music) to a measure of transcendence or, at least, detachment from the given order of things.

The Church As Exemplary Community: Despite all that has been said, and despite the doubts of some that the gates of hell may indeed have already given way as far as the church is concerned, I am not ready to abandon hope in the instrument of the church as a force for the reconstitution of human community. With all its faults, its cultural bondage and nostalgia for a dead past, timid leadership and lack of theological imagination, the church still displays a remarkable history of enduring and aiding in cultural transformation. This is not simply a matter of clever compromise and a knack for institutional survival. The church does have as a resource some basic clues as to the integrity of human community and the insanity of a community turned in on itself or devoted to past glories.

At its best the church from Pentecost onward has demonstrated something to the larger human community about its togetherness. It was together not on the basis of a common ideology or political program. Nor was it a mere collection of individuals supporting one another's creaturely needs and emotional handicaps. It was a community sharing a common experience of grace and living by a common hope. It exalted human interdependency in the "communion of the saints," the "body of Christ," the "one loaf" of the eucharistic assembly, a community united in the "our Father" and "the kingdom of God." This sense of a community has been severely eroded by Protestant individualism and Cartesian consciousness. Few assemblies of Christians have dared to think of their gathering as a model whereby other groups might find life a bit more open and hopeful. Our assemblies are too often "associations," too rarely "communities."

This condition of forced and artificial intimacy can be broken. And the church can learn from the counter culture what it means to be a people moving from an eroded culture to the breaking points of the future. It can learn risk and trust and a sense of hope. But the counter culture can learn something from the church as many of its instruments for change prove inadequate vehicles of the new culture: it can learn the wisdom of a community which finally understands that its life comes from beyond its own capacities and which is sustained by a determination to persist in the liberation of the oppressed and powerless and unimaginative. The church's hope goes beyond the success or failure of immediate political goals. It knows it often wins in losing.

This gracious wisdom was evident in an encounter of radical university students and two nuns engaged in nonviolent resistance to American policy in Indochina. Without strident voices or paranoid fears and with great humor and confidence, these two women instructed students in the strategies of a community that moves through the world not expecting to win every battle, yet knowing which way the future goes and being willing to dare to enter it. They reminded the students of a way into the future that the church had seemingly forgotten: trust the vision of the kingdom.

Increasingly, the persons who have made the decision to give their energies towards the possibility of a new cultural creation will look to Christians for a sign. They may again find in us a confidence that the gospel of liberation is what we both are about—or they may find us threatened and defensive, clinging to the old patterns and fearful of finding our own lives set in the context of a larger and more humane community.

5

COUNTER CULTURE
AND THE VISION
OF GOD

> Here between the hither and the farther shore
> While time is withdrawn, consider the future
> And the past with an equal mind.
> At the moment which is not of action or inaction
> You can receive this: 'on whatever sphere of being
> The mind of man may be intent
> At the time of death'—that is the one action
> (And the time of death is every moment)
> Which shall fructify in the lives of others:
> And do not think of the fruit of action.
> Face forward.
>
> —T. S. Eliot, *The Dry Salvages*

These pages have been written from the assumption that there *is* a deep and discernible shift in human consciousness behind the constellation of forces Roszak described as the counter culture and Reich celebrated as Consciousness III. It is counter in that it turns from the traditional sources of European culture and explicitly rejects the values of technocracy as dehumanizing. If California is something of a touchstone of the counter culture, then the Orient has replaced Europe as a source of wisdom. It also represents a turn from political conflict to the creation of alternate life styles.

The cultural gap in America is distinct from and more important than the generation gap or the political gap between liberal and conservative forces. At present, liberal reformers stand between the two cultures as mediators, but that role will become increasingly more difficult as the values of the old and new cultures clash. As with all cultural conflict, if the values of the new culture are basically contradictory to the old, compromise will no longer work, and one side or the other must triumph.

In opting for an alternate life style, the counter culture young have rejected many of the fundamental elements of Western civilization. They have also given us some clues as to the new sources they value and the models and meanings they find viable. Among these, there is the model of the primitive Christian movement, underground in character, maintaining an apocalyptic hope. This is not the first time that alienated groupings have identified with the Christian movement. Christians too easily have forgotten their beginnings as a counter culture contemptu-

ous of a proud and well-established culture. Roszak is not alone in pointing out the similarity
between the early Christian movement and the
counter culture.

> Hopelessly estranged by ethos and social class from
> the official culture, the primitive Christian commu-
> nity awkwardly fashioned of Judaism and the mys-
> tery cults a minority culture that could not but
> seem an absurdity to Greco-Roman orthodoxy. But
> the absurdity, far from being felt as a disgrace, be-
> came a banner of the community.[1]

While the contemporary church is viewed by the
counter culture as inextricably tied to the technocratic values of the prevailing culture, the
literature and music of the counter culture indicate that the Christian experience is a viable
model.

Counter Culture as Religion

There is a strong religious element in the diverse
expressions of the counter culture and, indeed,
the movement seems to represent for many of the
young a surrogate form of religion, a faith that
enables them to move beyond political despair.
Most often, they will reject the church not because of its essential gospel, but because of its
cultural bondage. They would find it possible
to identify with the mission of Jesus as he
announced it to Nazareth:

> The spirit of the Lord is upon me,
> because he has anointed me to preach good news to
>   the poor.
> He has sent me to proclaim release to the captives
>   and recovering of sight to the blind,
> to set at liberty those who are oppressed,
> to proclaim the acceptable year of the Lord.[2]

That is the message the alienated can hear: release from captivity, new sight for the blind, liberation for the oppressed. But beyond that point, things get murky and the young radicals especially have difficulty in making the connection between the mission of Jesus and the mission of the Christian church.

Instead, the counter culture advocates have attempted to put together those elements so torn asunder in the life of the church: apocalyptic hope and joyful play, a prophetic ethic and a mystical vision. Their vision of new cultural possibilities integrally relates politics and mysticism; it is no escapist vision. They are intent to press beyond the reductive rationalism of the academic establishment and the liberal reformism of the ecclesiastical establishment. Their mentors are visionaries: Herbert Marcuse and Norman O. Brown, Herman Hesse and Alan Watts. While brought up in the mainstream of behavioral psychology, they avidly turn to those with prophetic-mystic (that is to say, "religious") roots: Rollo May, Erich Fromm, Abraham Maslow, Erik Erikson, Alan Watts, R. D. Laing.

As a surrogate religion, the counter culture provides what the major religious traditions have offered in their originating power: a sense of distance from the given world, a shattering of an idolatrous framework of understanding, and a fresh appropriation of reality. The traditional understanding of religion has usually stressed the unitive, binding element. However, this does not do justice to the movement of separation and distance from the "world." For the Christian, this movement occurs in the proclamation of a new aeon being inaugurated in the kingdom of God. The world is considered "fallen"; it is viewed as restored through faith in the work and Lordship of Jesus Christ. For the Buddhist the world is seen as illusive and reconstituted through dissolution (samsāra and nirvāna). For the phenomenologist, the world is lost by the practice of epoché (the suspension of all norms) and regained through universal self-examination.

Driven by despair and a series of blocked possibilities, the creators and advocates of the counter culture have found relief in new means of perceiving their world and gaining necessary distance from it. They have learned from Norman O. Brown to respect "holy madness" and the authority of "second sight," an intensely personal vision in which miracles and revelation are possible and the old authorities are swallowed up in acts of new creation. They have turned to Herbert Marcuse for instruction in a political perspective that inverts the given political realities and sees possibilities for liberating communities from "repressive intolerance." In the same quest for distance and vision, they have turned to drugs, the *I Ching, Hare Krishna, The Tibetan Book of the Dead* and transcendental meditation.

In many ways, the counter culture appears to be now where the church was in the first century of its life: forging an underground existence against "the principalities and powers" of an oppressive state, purging itself of utopian fantasies and false visions, clarifying its language, constituting its symbols. It struggles with the conflict between violence and a peaceful change of consciousness; it experienced the gap between Woodstock and Altamont, and between mystic insight and occult witchcraft. It has produced a variety of communal styles and a rich body of music expressive of the new culture. Religious themes run through much of the new music, and while groups like the Rolling Stones seem to revel in satanic anarchy, the soft, hopeful side of the musical revolution now seems to be in the ascendency. The Beatles have embraced both Christian and Hindu elements in their songs, which deal with the illusive character of the objective world, the play of fantasy, the futility of political revolution. Folksingers such as Judy Collins and James Taylor have turned to songs that invoke Jesus as a potent metaphor against the powers of death. The rock opera, *Jesus Christ Superstar,* reveals the place the counter culture gives to Christ.

All of this is to indicate that Jesus is not left out of the movement toward a new culture. He is very much there—in the music, the icons, the faith of the counter culture. He is, however, more the Christ of Tolstoy or Dostoevski than the Christ of Billy Graham or Norman Vincent Peale. He is a proletarian friend, religious hero, exemplary figure of hope. But again, the young dissidents think they know where Christ is—in terms of the work of human liberation from a false consciousness. They would like to have the church as an ally if they sensed a struggle on the part of the church to deliver itself from cultural bondage.

What Role for Christians?

The last decade has been a painful one for the church. Again and again it has wrestled with its bondage to a restrictive cultural understanding. The civil rights movement, the Black Reparation demands, women's liberation, the divisive issue of America's Indochina policy—all have tested the freedom and will of Christians to speak for the kingdom of God as a transcendent reality shaping our decisions and engaging us in the task of liberation. Once more, the church is tested by the emerging counter culture. In many ways, it was easier for the church to respond to the civil rights movement—since that could be seen within the context of liberal reform—than to identify with the opposite values of the counter culture.

The counter culture cannot easily be absorbed by the church. It presents itself as an alien and threatening phenomenon in which central understandings of Western culture and Christian tradition are held in radical question: the nature of man, man's place in nature and history, the doctrine of revelation and redemption, the question of authority, and the character of the religious community. Our commitments are severely tested by such people as the Berrigans in burning draft records. Which do we value the most in a Christian culture: persons or property, technological requirements or human values? Furthermore, we find ourselves ill-equipped theologically to respond to the esoteric and mystic elements of the counter culture's new religion. The vigorous theological revival of the 1950s now seems parochial and inadequate.

In some ways, Paul Tillich's works seem to be the most helpful source. He was the theologian of culture, the apologist *par excellence*. His method of correlating theological symbol with existential questions, his psychotherapeutic sophistication, his love of the mystic tradition, his openness to Eastern religions—all seem to mark him as the one to follow. And, indeed, Tillich does remain a most seminal and provocative source of theological reflection on the surprising turns in our cultural history.

But Tillich remains a European Christian standing on boundaries that are not the boundaries of the young. However instructive and illuminating his systematic theology is, it is framed on the basis of a response to the secular world in which the Christian attempts to answer scientific and philosophical criticisms of Christian faith. The present situation finds us up against a new prophetic-mystic cultural matrix, a culture with the promise of the theonomous character Tillich valued as ideal.

He was bold enough in his last published lecture to indicate where he did envision the future of theology. It was in the direction of what he called "the Religion of the Concrete Spirit." [3] This meant for Tillich an examination of the elements of a culture and the way in which they point beyond themselves to the ultimate meaning of life. Theology, in this approach, would not deal with abstractions or systems, but with the depth experiences of human thought and action.

The builders of the new culture would also find

difficulty in interpreting their historic situation through Tillichian categories. Despite the flexibility of the "method of correlation," the accent remains on guilt and grace and a recovery of meaning before existential despair. While Tillich pioneered in a bold program of cultural renewal in the framework of religious socialism, his work was largely a response to the intellectual questions and social conditions of the late 19th century. Also, his ontological approach does not allow for a radical eschatology and worldly distance. Tillich's theology is a theology of courageous acceptance rather than a hopeful theology of liberation.

If this can be said of Tillich, a catholic and boundary-type theologian, the parochialism and inadequacies of Barth and the Niebuhrs seem all the greater. In a word, Protestant theology remains too bound to its European past and the intellectual horizon of the 19th century. It appears unprepared to speak out of a vision of spiritual depth for the liberation of those caught in cultural despair. Few have sensed the desperate yearnings of the new generation to fashion a religious faith that will give birth to new cultural creation. Martin Duberman, a historian and dramatist, speaks to this point:

> The great virtue of history, one the theatre stands in need of, is that it counteracts present-mindedness—the belief that what *is* has always been and must al-

ways be. To have historical perspective is to become aware of the range of human adaptability and purpose. Thus the ancient world (and the eighteenth century Enlightenment) saw man as a creature capable of using reason to perceive and follow "virtue"; the Christian view saw man capable of love as well as sin; the Renaissance believed that man's energy and will were sufficient to control both his personal destiny and his social environment.[4]

Does our present Christian worldview allow us to address ourselves convincingly to this crisis of hope? Do we find it possible to lay hold of theological resources appropriate for a time of cultural transformation? As Christians, will we identify with the basic thrust of the counter culture, or does our theology lead us to defensive justifications of the present culture?

Perhaps theology, as well as other academic disciplines, has fallen prey to what Roszak calls "the myth of objective consciousness" and thus suffers the reproach of the young who turn to magic, mystery, and the intuitive wisdom of the heart. Jacob Needleman, after surveying the widespread appeal of the new religions (Yoga, Zen, Meher Baba, etc.) for the American young, draws a similar but simpler conclusion:

Why is it that our popular established religions are so shaken in the face of the visible problems of our civilization: drugs, war, crime, social injustice, the breakdown of the family, the sexual revolution? Is it not because somewhere along the line belief took the place of faith for the majority of Jews and Christians? Faith cannot be shaken; it is the result of being shaken.[5]

A further diagnosis of the ills of Protestant theology is offered by one of the chief mentors of the counter culture, Norman O. Brown. Again, the fault is found in an inadequate eschatology, a deficient message of hope. Brown sees the genius of Luther's *theologia crucis* in affirming man's being in the world but not of it, and especially in Luther's capacity to balance the powers of death against the victory of Christ. The dominion of death and the devil is not evaded ("his craft and power are great"), but there is a bold confidence in God's rule and ultimate victory ("one little word shall fell him"). "It was only the mystical hope that made the realism psychologically bearable."[6]

Brown acknowledges the strength of the neo-orthodox revival in reaffirming this tension between demonism and eschatological hope and especially credits Paul Tillich with a convincing recovery of the demonic power, as well as a careful separation of the Christian message from cultural entanglements with an autonomous capitalism. But he faults Tillich and others for failing to deliver an equally compelling affirmation of the Christian hope. He sees the teaching of the Last Judgment, the Second Coming, and the kingdom of God subjected to a treatment of strained rationalism by the Protestant theologians. And he sees a persistent problem in the separation of grace and nature:

> As long as (to quote Tillich) "the Protestant principle cannot admit any identification of grace with a visible reality," and cannot repeat with conviction the tradition Christian faith that the time will come when grace will be made visible, and that this goal is the meaning of history, it looks as if neo-orthodox theology will remain incapable of casting out demons, and will therefore be of limited service to the life instinct in its war against the death instinct. It diagnoses but it does not cure.[7]

If these judgments ring true, then Christians have before them the prospect of recovering a fuller appropriation of their own heritage. The Christian symbols of hope and human liberation will be claimed by the larger human community, if not by the church. They will be appropriated by Marxists and mystics, by struggling communes and youthful musicians who are attracted to symbols and metaphors embarrassing to belief-ridden Christians.

Thus the counter culture not only presents Christians with the option of reclaiming elements of their faith long since abandoned; it likewise offers the option of moving beyond the European framework of Christian theology into a more universal expression of Christian faith. At both points, Christians will find themselves inhibited in their response. We are all too comfortable with the old securities. We would like to believe that the counter culture represents a romantic dream, ill-fated with youthful illusions. We see ourselves as representing the mature religion, knowing the perils of *hubris,* the ironies of history, the wisdom of human finitude. But that assumption will not serve the yearnings of the young. In their eyes, our "maturity" and "realism" are seen as cultural bondage.

Charles Reich may be wrong about many things, but he is not wrong when he points to the "ripeness" of our historical situation as it offers the possibility of a new life style.[8] There is unquestionably before us an open door into a new range of understanding and communal life. The Christian faith can be appropriated as an instrument of human liberation and Christian believers can shake loose from crippling dependencies and move into new cultural styles.

Let the argument for this possibility now focus on three immediate imperatives for the Christian community if it is to respond to the promise of the counter culture.

Toward a True Ecumenism: Beyond the West

If Christians mean what they say when they employ ecumenical language, they must show signs of moving theologically in that direction. They must conceive of their faith as "belonging to the whole inhabited world" in terms of faith experience at the depths and not belief systems in the abstract. As Harvard's Wilfrid C. Smith has so forcefully reminded us, Christian theology has scarcely begun to account *theologically* for the fact of human religious diversity. We have too often arrogantly or blindly pursued theology without taking into consideration the viability of traditions sustaining the allegiance of hundreds of millions of Buddhists and Moslems and Hindus. We have failed to meet them as our Lord met all men—in the anguish of love, in what Tillich called "The Religion of the Concrete Spirit." Wilfrid C. Smith, at the Center for the Study of World Religions, has exhibited a sympathetic imagination in raising for Christians the imperative of inter-faith understanding. He has exposed the artificiality of dealing with reified non-realities such as "Buddhism" or "Christianity" and suggested models for encountering the personal faith of men.[9] He calls us to engage ourselves with the qualitative adjective, "religious," rather than the abstract noun, "religion."

Paul Tillich also made some beginnings in this direction. He saw the dangers in attempting to create a religious synthesis of the great traditions (as sometimes suggested by Arnold Toynbee).

He knew that would be a synthetic universal concept, and he urged Christians to go another way:

> The way is to penetrate into the depths of one's own religion, in devotion, thought and action. In the depth of every living religion there is a point at which the religion itself loses its importance, and that to which it points breaks through its particularity, elevating it to spiritual freedom and with it to a vision of the spiritual presence in other expressions of the ultimate meaning of man's existence.[10]

The late Carl Michalson also provided a model for moving beyond European categories of theological reflection. His study of Japanese Christian theology pointed to quite original expressions of such traditional themes as atonement, church life, the interpretation of the Bible, and the Resurrection.[11] He expressed amazement and admiration for the ways in which Japanese Christians had treated questions largely ignored in the West, and he invited his theological colleagues to join the dialog.

The challenge, however, was not met. Protestants have continued to look to Europe for theological stimulation. A notable exception was Thomas J. J. Altizer, who some would not consider a church theologian but a historian of religion or literary critic. But that in itself says much about where the challenge has been met and the way in which the history of religion offers insight into Christian reflection. As a student of Mircea

Eliade at Chicago and a serious scholar of William Blake, Altizer blazed a new trail in his *Oriental Mysticism and Biblical Eschatology*.[12] He further pursued this theme in a provocative essay on "Nirvana and the Kingdom of God," in which he argued for a radical eschatology beyond Tillich's ontology and Barth's dialectic.[13] Once more, however, the argument was lost in the controversy over the "death-of-God," and few theologians have had either the grounding in the history of religion or the initiative to pursue the issue.

On the whole, Roman Catholics have been much more venturesome in pursuing serious theological dialog with the Eastern traditions. A survey of literature in the field will quickly confirm this judgment: Thomas Merton, *Mystics and Zen Masters;*[14] Heinrich Dumoulin, *A History of Zen Buddhism;*[15] Dom Aelred Graham, *Zen Catholicism* and *Conversations: Christian and Buddhist;*[16] Raymond Pannikar of Benares, who has taught at both Harvard Divinity and Union Theological in New York; R. C. Zaehner, *Mysticism: Sacred and Profane;*[17] and the prodigious efforts of the lay Catholic, Mircea Eliade, *Patterns in Comparative Religion*.[18] In terms of missionary scholarship, the Roman Catholics have established an enviable record and shown a greater capacity to deal with mystical, intuitive traditions.

148

In the meantime a host of critical issues wait to be explored if the Christian community is to participate in the formation of the counter culture. In its use of diverse religious elements, the counter culture has signalled the end of religious isolationism and called Christians to the task of formulating a more comprehensive religious vision. We are not called to create a synthetic theology, but a new life style. In the pursuit of that goal, our agenda of dialog must confront the following issues:

Selfhood. How do we understand human self-hood: as a substantial ego or as a fictitious illusion? What is at the core of human personality: a knowing self or a bundle of disguises and conditions (the Buddhist *Skandhas*)? Are people really as Buddhist folklore has portrayed them—like onions, with nothing at the core, except the tears of compassion? Is our true life history to be found in those moments of enlightenment and ecstasy—like a string of pearls without the string? Or is our life to be seen in a linear progression, linked in moments of time and set against the biblical drama of salvation? Does the process of salvation move *positively* toward the fulfillment of the self, toward the abundant life, perfection, maturity in Christ, or *negatively,* toward the extinction of desires, the dissolution of objective reality, the state of nirvana? What, after all, is the consequence of salvation for selfhood? Do we see the world differently? Are we freer, more compassionate creatures because of our vision of faith? Is there a critical distinction between the fruit of Buddhist enlightenment *(Prajñā,* intuitive wisdom, and *Karunā,* compassion) and Christian salvation *(pistis,* faith, and *agape,* sacrificial love)?

The Problem of Guilt. Does this remain the central existential problem of 20th century man? Are the theological formulas evolving out of the Reformation adequate to the binds experienced by the American youth? Could we not learn from the experience of Asian Christians something of the appeal and limitations of non-Western categories to the makers of the counter culture? What will it mean to our liturgies and ethics if we follow the lead of the theologians of hope in reversing the traditional assumption of Christian devotion?

> The thrust of devotion is not from natural to supernatural or from human to divine, but in reaching out to welcome the future of God's promise. The dynamic of Christian piety is the yearning for what is to be, not gratitude for past forgiveness.[19]

Is not the pull of the counter culture evident in just this division between those motivated by gratitude for past forgiveness—which *may* lead to cultural resignation—and those straining for the realization of a new future?

Nature: Are we prepared to rethink our recent bias against a theology of nature? Do we see the divine process of redemption including the realm of nature, or is history the sole arena of the drama of salvation? Do we not tend to make light of Jesus' admonition to "consider the lilies of the field" as an inappropriate guide to the resolution of human anxiety? Do we not separate the process theologians and the followers of Teilhard de Chardin from the faithful orthodoxy of biblical theologians? Are we sensitive to the dangers inherent in such phrases as "man's lordship over nature" or other such notions of stewardship? Especially important to dialog with the counter culture critics of Christian faith would be an awareness that some of these formulas were corrupted by 19th century Christian industrialists to justify the devastation of the environment. The young, in contrast, manifest a growing awareness of their intimate links with the natural world and question whether those who are alienated from nature can be trusted to exercise dominion.

The Character of the Sacred: Are we as Westerners not misled by the peculiar way in which we conceive the religious character of reality in terms of secular and sacred? The term *secularism* originated in Western Europe in the mid-19th century, its use generally referring to the deterioration of a cultural cohesiveness wherein ecclesiastical control prevailed. Nothing like that kind of distinction applies in the Eastern traditions. In India, for example, the division would be more along the lines of ordinary and extraordinary, mundane or supra-mundane, *Samsāra* (the cycle of rebirth) and *Brahma* (ultimate reality). The boundary line between the two is not a matter of belief or sociological participation; it is *moksa* (liberation).

Is there not much instruction to be found in the dramatic reversal of Harvey Cox's posture in *The Secular City* and his more recent, *Feast of Fools?* [20] While his treatise on secularization, under the tutelage of Reformed theology, spelled out the dimensions of the secularizing process, his more recent work has acknowledged the contrary values of the counter culture. Cox has now given his attention to the new shift: magic, militancy, mysticism, and festivity. The new movement resists the artificial dichotomy of secular and sacred. And here, Western Christians can learn from the East. The young who engage in the movement to the East are not proclaiming the end of religion; they are in search of a faith beyond the categories of Western Christianity.

Restoration of the Prophetic-Mystic Polarity

A second mandate raised by the counter culture involves the divorce effected in Reformed history of the prophetic and mystic elements in biblical faith. We *have* moved away from this tension and conceived our message as an "acoustical affair" generated out of hearing and believing rather than as a liberating vision enabling us to imagine new possibilities. The doctrine of justification has become the whole gospel under the dominance of neo-orthodoxy and has been used to justify liberal reform but not radical questioning of wasted cultural systems. The charge is usually raised from the neo-orthodox side that the mystic pole represents passivity and escape from the burdens of history. But the new visionaries do not see the mystic vision as leading to private *gnosis* or passive retreat, but rather the beginning point of more perceptive social strategies.

At this point, the Protestant experience represents an impoverished spirituality and a truncated expression of Christian faith. Thomas Altizer's judgment of some years ago was not heard in the churches: that we have distorted our faith into an intellectual treatment of the idea of God and lost the transcendent, immediate dimension. He revealed "the nakedness of the theologians" (Barth, Bultmann, and Tillich) in failing to witness to a liberating faith. All were judged as having failed to present the Christian life as a perspective from which one could stand apart from world and cultural limits.

As Protestants committed to a theology of the Word, we have severed ourselves from the tradition of the early church:

> Before the first of our extant creeds had assumed its present shape—before any dominant liturgical forms had emerged from the primitive fluidity of worship—before so much as the bare terminology of the great Christological controversies had entered the new vocabulary—before it was certain whether "the Word" or "the Son of God" should be the crowning title of the Risen Lord—before even the propriety of speaking of the Godhead as a Trinity had become apparent—before the Church had passed a single one of these milestones in her history, the first of a great line of post-apostolic theologians, Irenaeus, had declared: "The glory of God is a living man; and the life of man is the vision of God." [21]

This dimension of our faith has been kept in the history books. We have located the transcendent and ineffable character of the divine in our creeds and theologies and biblical sources. We have become word-bound and rationally restricted. We have closed our minds and hearts to those moments in which theological systems are eclipsed by mystic insight. Protestants would do well to remember the experience of the major theologian of the medieval church, Thomas Aquinas, who wrote in his *Summa contra Gentiles:* "For then alone do we know God truly, when we believe that He is far above all that man can possibly think of God." Aquinas later found that these were not casual words when, during a

Mass in the chapel of St. Nicholas at Naples, he was struck by a rapture of the mind and determined that he would write no more.

The recovery of the mystic side of Christian faith need not spell the end of theology, but it does portend the necessity of a new theological style, a posture of theological reflection that is close to meditation. It is a style pursued by the late Thomas Merton, especially in his encounter with Zen Buddhist tradition. Merton knew that Zen could not be grasped through the usual theological tools; it demanded that one encounter its quite distinctive art forms, its suprising spiritual disciplines, and its radical absurdities.

> Zen is not theology, and it makes no claim to deal with theological truth in any form whatever. Nor is it an abstract metaphysic. It is, so to speak, a concrete and lived ontology which explains itself not in theoretical propositions but in acts emerging out of a certain quality of consciousness and awareness.[22]

Merton's characterization of Zen can almost be taken as a paradigm of the promise of a new theological style related to the new consciousness and the new mysticism.

The barriers impeding such a movement are considerable. We are conditioned by more than four centuries of Protestant history to lean more heavily on the prophetic side and maintain a suspicion of the mystic side. We will not easily open ourselves to instruction from either the counter culture or Eastern, non-Christian sources. Thomas Altizer pressed hard at this point: "A major task of contemporary theology is that of recovering—or should we say creating—an eschatological vision of God, and it is just at this point that Buddhism has a deep relevance to our task." [23] The Buddhist understanding of nirvana—a reality absolutely unrelated to any other reality—suggested for Altizer the possibility of recovering radical transcendence through taking the power of the kingdom of God seriously: "to know God apart from his Kingdom is to know a God who is a God only of *this* world, and never the God proclaimed by Jesus Christ." [24] Furthermore, Altizer argued for a more radical and mystic appropriation of the kingdom of God, not as an act of withdrawal from social responsibility but as a means of gaining worldly distance before the new world could be seen out of the reality of the kingdom of God. Altizer spoke as a cultural revolutionary, dissatisfied with H. Richard Niebuhr's notion of the kingdom of God as "transformed culture" or Paul Tillich's "Unconditional Ground." He called Christians to a vision in which "the world appears in a new light, for now the world gives witness to its ultimate end, when the world will be transfigured by a New Creation, when God will be all in all." [25]

It appears that the experience of the counter culture in perceiving the dead ends of reform liberalism may parallel the experience of many Christians as they see the inadequacies of a tradition that has lost the tension between prophetic and mystic elements. Tired liberals in both camps confess that prophetic action cannot be sustained without the vision of new styles of ministry. If we are to serve as helpful resources in the making of the counter culture, this tension must be restored.

A Community of Cultural Revolutionaries

A third mandate will face the Christian community with the painful task of reexamining its readiness to join the coalition of counter culture forces—for honest dialog, at the least. As noted earlier, this will mean that we attempt to separate Christian essentials from the cultural trappings of 20 centuries and also learn to distinguish between theology as a vehicle for expressing our faith and theology as a substitute for the vision of faith.

Apart from this internal task of cultural purgation and faithful regeneration, how prepared are we to open ourselves to the witness of the counter culture? Do we perceive the necessity of cultural idols being shattered? Are we willing to risk experiments with new life styles? How close are we as a people to the despair of the young or the "burnt-out cases" of liberal reformists? How sensitive are we to those who live at the margins of society and see us as bearers of a cultural gospel, justifying oppression and unwilling to speak on behalf of the powerless? Can we identify with the desperation that leads Christians into civil disobedience and directly challenge the values of a technological culture?

These are not rhetorical questions. Viable responses will be painful and costly. The church will experience both a generation gap and a cultural gap at every point in which it tries to relate to the energies of the counter culture—whether it tries to free its evangelism from the snares of Madison Avenue techniques or questions a social-political ministry of reconciliation that does not mean justice but reform. It will also mean reshaping our liturgies and providing pastoral counseling that does not end with individual comfort but deals with the causes of distress.

The Christian church, when it is faithful to its Lord, acknowledges that it is a way, but not the source of human renewal. It is a meeting place for the world's anguish and God's love, a love that leads us into new creation. It is a community wherein all of our separate and collective ideologies are shared and tested over against the vision of Christ. That vision is a vision of the New

Aeon, the kingdom of God, a reign in which the original promise of creation will be fulfilled. It is not a utopia or political program; it is not a disposition or moral motivation in the heart of man. It is rather God's initiative, a seminal beginning in which seeds of intuition and revelation must ever be cultivated through disciplines of spiritual care. As the Gospel parables teach, the kingdom of God is that presence in the midst of the human enterprise qualifying human life— not "beyond" but in our midst as "seed" (Mark 4:26), "leaven" (Luke 13:20), a "hidden treasure" (Matthew 13:44), a "net" gathering every kind (Matthew 13:46). Those of great wealth find it hard to enter, whereas children enter most naturally. Children and those broken in life (the lame and the blind, prostitutes and tax-collectors) will enter before the religious establishment and the culturally secure (scribes, Pharisees, priests).

The communities that witness to the reality of the kingdom of God will be given the task of nurturing fresh forms of consciousness that are generated out of the kingdom beyond culture. They will stand beyond the present cultural binds and, like Gregory of Nyssa and St. Paul, strain forward, "forgetting what lies behind." The way of *epekstasis* means strain and risk; it means facing forward. It means remembering with Kierkegaard that there are no analogies available for the coming of the new, only contradictions and ambiguities before which we must choose.

There are those who have shown the way: Robert Kennedy, in the political arena, broke with the old reform formulas; Martin Luther King and the Berrigan brothers, in the church, opted for new strategies and coalitions. All were sustained by a dream or vision that enabled them to move against the dead weight of the past into the face of hostility, misunderstanding, and death. Such people leaned heavily into the future with an expectancy of something new being realized. As Dr. King preached on the eve of his death in Memphis, he sounded such a note: "I have seen the promised land. I may not get there with you. But it doesn't matter now. We as a people will get to the promised land. My eyes have seen the glory of the coming of the Lord!"

Vision for the Christian community need not be understood as an uncritical identification with the diverse visions of the counter culture. Some are demonic and illusive. However, the church can serve as a bridge between the cultures and between the generations. It can maintain a posture of critical openness to both established culture and counter culture and test the promises of both against the formative power of a transcendent Gospel. The church can join all who engage in a critique of the violence technocratic values exercise over human needs. It can help its older and more conservative members to understand the conflict of values and the connection between Christian commitment and cultural loyalties. Above all, it can help its members understand that it is not the young alone who resist the depersonalizing force of technocracy. Young and old alike have sensed the insanity of America's Indochina policy. North Carolina's crusty 74-year-old Senator Sam Ervin joined youthful opponents of the proposed computer data bank on security information with words that reveal a Christian base. He stated that the new technology "has removed the quality of mercy from our institutions by making it impossible to forget, to forgive, to understand, to tolerate." [26]

In exercising such a bridge ministry, the church must increasingly question efforts at reform that are likely to reinforce a society directed by technocratic values. With issues of war and ecology and expenditures of great sums for space exploration or arms, Christian people must find their voice. It will mean learning the difference between tinkering with a faulty system and being willing to pay the price for a new one. It is the difference between Niebuhr's "Christian realism" and the new theology of hope. It is the difference between adopting the posture of iconoclast and rebel on the one hand, and opting for the vision, radicality, and persistency of the true revolutionary on the other. In this regard, the Christian life is *always* counter cultural and *always* revolutionary.

In pursuit of revolutionary goals, Christians need not become romantic utopians or political subversives. They can, however, give themselves to a revolution of consciousness and draw on the considerable resources of their faith. At this point in our history, the choices are many and even at our most perceptive, we still "see through a glass darkly." The future is undetermined; only history as shaped in our collective destiny will decide. The counter culture for the moment remains as described by Roszak, a rough constellation populated by "technocracy's children," moving away from the politics and religion of their fathers. Through its many failures, abortive drug "trips," and mystical quests, something is trying to be born and we are all witnesses to the travail of new birth and the promise of a real advent. If there is a final word said, let it be the simple and revolutionary clue from the Gospels:

> And no one puts a piece of unshrunk cloth on an old garment, for the patch tears away from the garment, and a worse tear is made. Neither is new wine put into old wineskins; if it is, the skins burst, and the wine is spilled, and the skins are destroyed; but new wine is put into fresh wineskins, and so both are preserved.[27]

NOTES

Chapter 1

1. See especially, Edgar Z. Friedenberg, *The Vanishing Adolescent* (New York: Dell Publishing, 1959); Paul Goodman, *Growing Up Absurd* (New York: Vintage Books, 1962); Kenneth Keniston, *The Uncommitted; Alienated Youth in American Society* (New York: Delta Books, 1965); *Young Radicals* (New York: Harcourt, Brace & World, 1968).

2. Theodore Roszak, *The Making of a Counter Culture* (New York: Doubleday Anchor, 1969).

3. *Ibid.*, p. xii.

4. Charles Reich, *The Greening of America* (New York: Random House, 1970).

5. *Ibid.*, p. 311.

6. *Ibid.*, p. 316.

7. *Ibid.*, p. 395.

8. *The Christian Science Monitor*, December 15, 1970, Section 2, p. 1.

9. Peter and Brigitte Berger, "The Eve of the Bluing of America," *The New York Times*, February 15, 1971, p. 23.

163

10. *The Christian Advocate,* March 4, 1971, p. 3.

11. Lewis Mumford, *The Myth of the Machine:* Vol. I. *Technics and Human Development* (New York: Harcourt, Brace, & Jovanovich, 1967); and Vol. II. *The Pentagon of Power* (New York: Harcourt, Brace, & Jovanovich, 1970).

12. Gerald Holton, *New York Times Book Review,* December 13, 1970, p. 2.

13. Lewis Mumford, *The Pentagon of Power,* Plate #26, following p. 340.

14. *Ibid.,* p. 462.

15. "Who'll Stop the Rain?", by John C. Fogerty, Credence Clearwater Revival, BMI, 1969.

16. Larry L. King, *Harper's,* "Blowing My Mind at Harvard," October, 1970, p. 98.

17. See Tom Wolfe's *The Electric Kool Aid Acid Test* (New York: Bantam Books, 1969).

Chapter 2

1. J. D. Salinger, *Franny and Zooey* (Boston: Little, Brown and Co., 1961), p. 39.

2. See especially Marcel's *The Mystery of Being* (Chicago: Henry Regnery Co., 1960).

3. William James, *The Varieties of Religious Experience* (New York: Modern Library, 1902), pp. 371-372.

4. Anne Freemantle, ed., *The Protestant Mystics,* Introduction by W. H. Auden (New York: New American Library, 1964).

5. *Ibid.,* p. 26.

6. See Denis De Rougemont's *Love in the Western World* (New York: Doubleday Anchor Books, 1957). Especially, "Orthodox Mystics and the Language of Passion," p. 154 ff.

7. From *The Cloud of Unknowing,* author unknown. F. C. Happold, *Mysticism* (Baltimore: Penguin Books, 1963), p. 277.

8. Freemantle, p. 20.

9. Rudolf Otto, *The Idea of the Holy* (New York: Oxford Galaxy Press, 1958), p. 206.

10. James Clark, *The Great German Mystics* (Oxford: Blackwell, 1949), p. 48.

11. *Signposts to Perfection: A Selection from the Sermons of Johann Tauler*, edited by Elizabeth Strakosch (St. Louis and London: 1958), pp. 131-132.

12. Susanna Winkworth, ed., *The History and Life of John Tauler With Twenty-five of His Sermons* (London: Smith, Elder and Company, 1857), p. 202.

13. Henry O. Taylor, *Thought and Experience in the Sixteenth Century*, Vol. I (New York: Macmillan Company, 1920), p. 195.

14. Otto, p. 103.

15. *Ibid.*, p. 104.

16. John Emory, ed., *The Works of The Rev. John Wesley*, Vol. V (New York: Carlton and Porter, 1871), p. 694.

17. Karl Barth, *The Epistle to the Romans* (London: Oxford University Press, 1933), p. 316.

18. Reinhold Niebuhr, *The Self and the Dramas of History* (New York: Scribners, 1951), p. 64.

19. Richard Rubenstein, *Playboy*, "Judaism and the Death of God," July, 1967.

20. Erik Erikson, *Young Man Luther* (New York: Norton, 1958).

21. Jacob Needleman, *The New Religions* (New York: Doubleday, 1970).

22. Egon Schwarz, "Herman Hesse, The American Youth Movement, and the Problems of Literary Evaluation," *PMLA*, October, 1970, p. 977 f.

23. *Steppenwolf* (New York: Bantam Books, 1969), p. 24.

24. *Ibid.*, p. 41.

25. *Ibid.*, pp. 154-155.

26. *Siddartha* (New York: New Directions, 1957), p. 111.

27. *Ibid.*, p. 138.

28. For a helpful understanding of this basic characteristic of Eastern thought, see Hajime Nakamura's *Ways of Thinking of Eastern Peoples*, especially Chapter 3, "Preference for the Negative" (Honolulu: East-West Center Press, 1964).

29. *Siddartha*, p. 141.

30. *Steppenwolf*, pp. 72-73.

31. *Ibid.*, p. 68.

32. *Ibid.*, p. 69.

33. *The Glass Bead Game* (New York: Bantam Books, 1970), pp. xiv-xv.

34. *Ibid.,* p. 290.

35. *Ibid.,* p. 291.

36. *Ibid.,* p. 327.

37. *Ibid.,* p. 151.

38. *Ibid.,* p. 334.

39. Paul Tillich, *Systematic Theology,* Volume I (Chicago: University of Chicago Press, 1951), p. 140.

40. *Ibid.*

41. Tillich, *Systematic Theology,* Volume III, p. 242.

Chapter 3

1. *The Greening of America,* p. 305.

2. *Ibid.,* p. 346.

3. Sir Kenneth Clark, *Civilisation* (New York: Harper and Row, 1969), p. 320.

4. Reich, p. 347.

5. Lewis Mumford, *The Pentagon of Power,* pp. 422-423.

6. *Ibid.,* p. 433.

7. Alan Watts, *The Book* (New York: Collier Books, 1967), p. 101.

8. Thomas Merton, "The Self of Modern Man and the New Christian Consciousness," Montreal, *The R. M. Bucke Memorial Society Newsletter-Review,* 1266 Pine Ave. West, Montreal, Quebec). Vol. 11, No. 1, April 1967, p. 17.

9. Thomas Merton, *Contemplative Prayer* (New York: Doubleday Image Books, 1971), p. 116.

10. Thomas Merton, *Mystics and Zen Masters* (New York: Farrar, Straus and Giroux, 1967), p. 26.

11. Merton, "The Self of Modern Man and the New Christian Consciousness," p. 18.

12. *Ibid.*

13. *Ibid.*

14. *Ibid.,* p. 20.

15. Karl Jaspers, *Man in the Modern Age* (New York: Doubleday Anchor Books, 1951), p. 215.

16. *Ibid.,* p. 216.

17. Philippians 3:13-14, RSV.

Chapter 4

1. The Port Huron Statement is included in Mitchell Cohen and Dennis Hale's, *The New Student Left* (Boston: Beacon Press, 1967), p. 13.

2. *The Making of a Counter Culture,* p. 55.

3. See Ferdinand Tönnies, *Community and Society* (1957) and *From Max Weber: Essays in Sociology,* ed. by H. H. Gerth and C. Wright Mills (1946).

Chapter 5

1. *The Making of a Counter Culture,* p. 43.

2. Luke 4:18, RSV.

3. See Paul Tillich, *The Future of Religions* (New York: Harper and Row, 1966), p. 90 f.

4. Martin Duberman, *The Uncompleted Past* (New York: Random House, 1969), pp. 31-32.

5. Jacob Needleman, *The New Religions* (New York: Doubleday, 1970), p. 223.

6. Norman O. Brown, *Life Against Death* (New York: Vintage Books, 1959), p. 223.

7. *Ibid.,* p. 224.

8. *The Greening of America,* pp. 3-20.

9. See especially W. C. Smith, *The Faith of Other Men* (New York: Mentor Books, 1965), and *The Meaning and End of Religion* (New York: Mentor Books, 1964).

10. Paul Tillich, *Christianity and the Encounter of the World Religions* (New York: Columbia University Press, 1963), p. 97.

11. Carl Michalson, *Japanese Contributions to Christian Theology* (Philadelphia: Westminster Press, 1960).

12. Thomas J. J. Altizer, *Oriental Mysticism and Biblical Eschatology* (Philadelphia: Westminster Press, 1961).

13. Thomas J. J. Altizer, "Nirvana and the Kingdom of God," *New Theology No. 1* (New York: Macmillan, 1964), p. 150 f.

14. Thomas Merton, *Mystics and Zen Masters* (New York: Farrar, Straus and Giroux, 1967).

15. Heinrich Dumoulin, S.J., *A History of Zen Buddhism* (New York: McGraw-Hill, 1965)

16. Dom Aelred Graham, *Zen Catholicism* (New York: Harcourt, Brace and World, 1963); and *Conversations: Christian and Buddhist* (New York: Harcourt, Brace, & Jovanovich, 1968).

17. R. C. Zaehner, *Mysticism: Sacred and Profane* (New York: Oxford University Press, 1961). Zaehner includes a delightful account of his own experience with LSD.

18. Mircea Eliade, *Patterns in Comparative Religion* (New York: Meridian Books, 1963).

19. Richard Neuhaus, "Wolfhart Pannenberg: Profile of a Theologian," in Pannenberg's *Theology and the Kingdom of God* (Philadelphia: Westminster Press, 1969), p. 40.

20. *Feast of Fools* (Cambridge, Mass.: Harvard University Press, 1969).

21. Kenneth E. Kirk, *The Vision of God* (London and New York: Longmans Green, 1934), pp. 1-2.

22. Merton, *Mystics and Zen Masters,* p. ix.

23. Thomas J. J. Altizer, "Nirvana and the Kingdom of God," p. 162.

24. *Ibid.,* p. 163.

25. *Ibid.,* pp. 165-166.

26. *The Charlotte Observer,* December 20, 1970, Section 1, p. 1.

27. Matthew 9:16-17.